Lovely Bits of Old England

John Betjeman

Lovely Bits of Old England

Selected Writings from
𝕿𝖍𝖊 𝕿𝖊𝖑𝖊𝖌𝖗𝖆𝖕𝖍

Edited by
Gavin Fuller

First published in Great Britain
2012 by Aurum Press Ltd
7 Greenland Street
London NW1 0ND
www.aurumpress.co.uk

ISBN 978 1 78131 012 0

1 3 5 7 9 10 8 6 4 2
2012 2014 2016 2015 2013

Typeset in Mrs Eaves by Saxon Graphics Ltd, Derby
Printed by MPG Books, Bodmin, Cornwall

Contents

Introduction

John Betjeman (1906-84) created, as Wordsworth said all great and original writers must, the taste by which he was relished. That was the view in 1984 of the substantial obituary that the *Daily Telegraph* devoted to this quirky figure, who had grown, from a fringe advocate of the outmoded and outlandish in architecture and poetry, into a familiar and much loved presence on the television, saying things with which many viewers agreed about the threatened beauties of the British countryside and townscapes.

'Not since Tennyson has a poet won such renown,' said Philip Larkin, and what's more Betjeman sold. His *Collected Poems*, published in 1958, sold 1,000 copies a week and soon reached sales of 100,000. Yet, in 1961, Betjeman still felt able to say: 'I will be completely forgotten in five years from now.' No forecast could have been less accurate. He had turned into a national treasure, and his columns in the *Telegraph*, written mainly in the 1950s and 1960s, played a large part in the process. Today those pieces are as readable as ever, having the added fascination of historical perspective.

How well they are written, too. In every one, the reader catches the authentic voice of Betjeman. There is no slapdash hackery here. The well-stocked mind, which astonished television audiences by recognising the most recondite corners of old England, made historical and social connections where others saw only change and decay. Each article is a slice of mature Betjeman, fresh from the oven. Take his piece from 1958 on the muddle of street furniture invading the centres of historic towns. In Burford and Birkenhead, Marlborough and Newcastle he saw the mess made by concrete lamp standards, traffic signs and bus shelters, and he found out who was to blame. He even discovered that local authority sanitary engineers put up signs 'Men' and 'Women' or 'Ladies' and 'Gents', 'Lavatory' or 'Convenience' according to the social status of the area.

John Betjeman began reviewing books for the *Daily Telegraph* in 1951, moving from the left-wing *Daily Herald* with no discernible lurch in his style or expressed opinions. In 1958 he began his architectural column in the paper, called 'Men and Buildings', a title that reflected the humanity of the lens through which he surveyed not isolated structures but stone and brick for living and working in town and country. In the *Spectator*, which he now left behind, he had written a similar weekly column under the title 'City and Suburban'. This was a quotation, or almost a quotation, from *Paradise Regained*, where Milton speaks of Athens, 'hospitable in her sweet recess / City or Suburban, studious walks and shades'. Not wishing to let a good title wither, the affable Christopher Fildes later adopted 'City and Suburban' for his celebrated column in the same magazine on the City of London and business.

When Betjeman began reviewing for the *Telegraph*, its literary editor was E.C. Bentley. A childhood friend of G.K. Chesterton, Bentley had given his middle name to the verse-form the 'clerihew' ('George the Third / Ought never to have occurred. / One can only wonder / At so grotesque a blunder.'). Himself the author of an evergreen whodunnit, *Trent's Last Case*, Bentley was universally liked by his colleagues at the paper and the authors with whom he had dealings. Not so his successor from 1956, H.D. Ziman, a good-natured man but, according to Duff Hart-Davis, the historian of the *Telegraph*, 'one of the greatest bores ever to send people fleeing down the corridors'. He was said to have been appointed literary editor only because Colin Coote, the editor, could no longer bear his contributions to the leader-writers' conferences.

In 1957, the *Telegraph* books pages were lucky enough to carry Betjeman's review, here reprinted, of an extraordinary novel by his friend of several decades Evelyn Waugh. *The Ordeal of Gilbert Pinfold*, Betjeman revealed, was 'about a middle-aged Roman Catholic novelist going mad' — Waugh himself. Betjeman recognised a masterpiece of novelistic self-revelation, but, unlike other such works, 'readable, thrilling and detached'. He was also sufficiently brave to admit that in Waugh's account he saw something of himself reflected. 'Almost any age,' Betjeman had written elsewhere, 'seems civilised except that in which I live.' It was the same for the novel's protagonist: Pinfold 'dislikes the wireless and the people it employs, Picasso, plastics, sunbathing and jazz — "everything in fact that had happened in his own life-time".' During a sea voyage alone, Pinfold, who is 'under the impression that he is fundamentally amiable and gentlemanly', begins to hear voices: 'all the sorts of people he doesn't like conspiring to persecute him. He hears his most intimate shames discussed.' Betjeman asks: 'Is this novel or autobiography? It is certainly a picture of hell on earth.' Then he says something very striking: 'I have an idea that most of us are haunted by voices such as these. I know that in times of depression I hear arguments such as Mr Waugh describes going on in my head.'

In 1964, Betjeman became a contributor to the new *Telegraph* colour magazine, which came out with the Friday paper, not on Sundays. It was edited for twenty-two years, with astonishing tenacity, by the tyrannical John Anstey, who, it seemed to his employees, often sent them alarming memos on the eve of their summer holidays. Betjeman, always anxious about the quality of his own work, was not the sort of writer to benefit from the editorial criticisms and suggestions that Anstey encouraged his staff to make about contributors' copy. Yet Betjeman continued to produce good pieces for what by 1969 he was calling 'the hateful *Daily Telegraph* Magazine', which was paying him a very useful £2,500 a year, plus £500 expenses.

Throughout his years with the *Telegraph*, Betjeman was able to fight some of his rear-guard actions to save buildings with which he is now associated: the successful battle to save St Pancras Station and the Midland Grand Hotel, the heroic failure to save the Euston Arch, or propylaeum. The very failure to stop the demolition of that Doric portico outside Euston station — even the rejection of the contractor's offer to number the stones so that it might be re-erected on a different site — won followers for Betjeman's way of thinking about conservation.

It is all the more intriguing, then, to see an article from 1965 on the unregarded architecture of Customs Houses. For one of Betjeman's less remembered defeats was the campaign three years earlier to save from demolition the Coal Exchange, a splendid Victorian iron rotunda in Lower Thames Street, London. One counter-proposal that Betjeman favoured was to shave off part of the nearby Custom House instead, to allow for the proposed road widening. In his *Telegraph* article, while ostensibly praising the unexpected splendour and charm of neo-Classical Customs Houses, such as those in Greenock and Leith, he writes of the 'safe, unoriginal brothers Robert and Sydney Smirke', who rebuilt the London Custom House in the 1820s.

The changes that have continued to transform Britain's historic towns since Betjeman's day give added interest to many of his observations. His engaging survey of Birmingham in 1961 mentions Augustus Pugin's design for 'the soaring, impressive and thin Roman Catholic Cathedral of St Chad (1839) and its Bishop's House'. What he mourns is the damage done to the city by traffic: 'The motor car has strangled Birmingham, congesting its centre despite an ingenious one-way traffic system'. Since then, the Bishop's House has been demolished to make way for a ring-road, on which traffic roars past the very steps of the cathedral, cutting it off like a Chinese Wall.

In a walk down the Strand in London in 1967, Betjeman laments that at Ludgate Circus, 'the railway bridge kills the famous view of St Paul's across from the bottom of Ludgate Hill'. This was the line to Ludgate Hill station, built for the London, Chatham, and Dover

Railway and closed in 1929. Perhaps in another mood, Betjeman would have regretted its loss. The bridge, he noted, had been made solid where its parapet had once been of open trelliswork. That was the view depicted in a Gustave Doré engraving of 1872, showing a bedlam of horse-drawn traffic below the bridge, across which a train passes, belching smoke. The bridge was demolished in 1990, and a building about which Betjeman complained, shouldering into the West façade of the cathedral, has also been replaced, along with the 1960s iniquities of Paternoster Square. 'More damage,' he remarked, 'has been done to London and our other old towns by "developers" and their tame architects than ever was done by German bombing.' What Betjeman would make of the new Paternoster Square – incorporating Temple Bar, brought back from its century of rustication in Hertfordshire to act as a gateway, or perhaps a propylaeum like the lost arch of Euston – we should very much like to know.

The nation could now, more than ever, do with the acute observations of this engaging, vastly knowledgeable, self-deprecating, untidy, poetic, slightly boozy figure, full of laughter and melancholy. Instead we are consoled in taking pleasure from the rich haul recovered by Gavin Fuller with loving diligence from the bedrock of past volumes of the *Telegraph*.

Christopher Howse
London
September 2012

*What will it be
like now the
'developers' are in?*
Betjeman's
Britain

૭૦૦૪

On 25 September 1964 the *Daily Telegraph* became the first daily newspaper to publish a magazine, doing so every Friday. John Betjeman was one of the earliest writers to move over from the newspaper to the new supplement, taking advantage of its scope for increased word count and glossier presentation to create a new series of articles, 'Betjeman's Britain', which first appeared in the second issue and promised to examine 'the splendours and miseries of British architecture.' Given the architectural magnificence of various towns and cities around the British Isles Huddersfield makes for an interesting, and certainly not the most obvious, choice to open this series, which over the next year or so developed a quirky look at aspects of British architecture, sometimes concentrating on place, at others themes. Betjeman scholars and newspaper archivists were not well served by the magazine soon dropping 'Betjeman's Britain' as a heading, as it becomes unclear whether later articles fall into this series, but here is a selection which shows the whole span of these pieces, from town studies to histories of types of building, and even a visit to an island to round things off.

Huddersfield Discovered

2 October 1964

৪০ ୦୫

A hot day in summer is the time to explore the industrial cities of the North. Preferably, it should be holiday time for then the architecture reveals itself. On working days everybody is too busy and every street has its hideous frill of parked cars.

Stand in Greenhead Park, Huddersfield, on a fine Sunday afternoon. The park was opened in 1884 so that trees are well-grown and the ample nineteenth-century style of landscape gardening survives, with winding walks and vistas. The flower beds are delightfully Victorian with no signs of our niggling age of gnomes and bird baths. The brass band is playing in the white and green bandstand. Lobelias and begonias gleam in municipal borders. A floral emblem on a slope of lawn commemorated the anniversary of the Federation of Professional Business Women's Clubs (Huddersfield Branch). Kiddiz are splashing in the kiddi-pool. The Boer War Memorial, which is a statue of a soldier, rises among geranium beds where paths of asphalt intersect. The door of the conservatory bangs shut for a hundredth time and lets a family out of tropical forest into our northern clime. Under the dusty August-looking trees, fathers play catch with their children. This many peopled park is no place for lovers. It is a place for families. Indian ladies in saris, with their husbands, add colour to the scene. Gaunt against the western sky rise the classical columns of the memorial to the 1914 war.

From Greenhead Park here in the centre of the town one can look down to the wooded valleys with their stone-built mills and chimneys which gave the town prosperity, first from spinning worsted and now from engineering and chemicals as well. Engineering goes with mill machinery so that famous gear makers and motor accessory firms are in the town. Dyeing goes with worsted, hence the chemicals.

Huddersfield has much beautiful and unregarded architecture. A century ago, when its limestone buildings were white and new, it was described as 'the handsomest mill town in Yorkshire', a sort of Athens on the steep slopes of the River Colne, with a few Gothic churches and the pinnacled Huddersfield College (1838) to add variety to the scene. Huddersfield tells its story so clearly in its buildings that before all trace of the older work is gone under the bulldozer let us have a look.

All along the valleys of the rivers Colne and Holme and the lesser brooks which pour brown waters down from the Yorkshire moors are villages where weaving was an industry done by hand in the top storeys of cottages. Many of these cottages survive from the seventeenth and eighteenth centuries. You can tell them by the rows of oblong windows set close together on first and second floors. They look like old-fashioned double-decked tram cars made of brown brick and stone. Here whole families took advantage of the daylight, which is why these cottages are generally high up, and wove the famous Yorkshire worsted. Even in the commercial centre of Huddersfield itself, in the noted, and now doomed, yard of the Pack Horse Hotel, there is part of a weaver's cottage. Outlying villages like Stainland, Oldfield, Outlane and Hepworth have more of them to show. From these villages the hand loom weavers brought their cloth by packhorse first to the market at Almondbury, a hill-top village west of Huddersfield with a large Perpendicular church and old grammar school. Almondbury today is the sort of semi-rural place where commuters live and is to Huddersfield what Sutton Coldfield is to Birmingham. It retains its ancient character.

In 1671 the Ramsden family, the baronets of Longley Hall, on the Huddersfield side of the parish, obtained a licence to hold a cloth market in the churchyard of Huddersfield down in the valley. Huddersfield prospered, Almondbury waned. In 1768 a beautiful oval top-lit Cloth Hall was built at the top of the new town. This made the place the centre of the cloth market for many miles. The Corporation destroyed this splendid building in 1930 and a ponderous cinema was erected on the site. The elegant white wood cupola and some of the old brick walls of the Cloth Hall have been put up in Ravensknowle Park where they challenge comparison with the nearby Victorian Italianate mansion which is now a museum.

From wherever you approach the town today the mills of Georgian and Victorian times are most in evidence. Water power and water transport changed the district. Sir John Ramsden's canal, now being filled in, connected it with the Calder and Hebble navigation to the north. Another canal connected it with Ashton and Oldham, to the south-west. The swift Yorkshire streams drove the new machinery for weaving worsted. Bitter was the resentment of the hand loom weavers in the cottages on the hills, as the valley farmers prospered with their mills. There were Luddite agitations.

These earlier mills in the valleys are all handsome buildings, oblong with many rows of plain windows, proportioned to the wall space with that instinctive sense of scale to be found in all our industrial builders until this century. Sometimes a mill owner, copying Arkwright at Cromford in Derbyshire, tried to make his mill look like a country house of enormous size, a sort of Chatsworth but in a Yorkshire valley setting of sycamore, ash, oak and beech.

At Longwood, Gothic has been attempted and a Georgian mill has a battlemented top. Near the confluence of the Holme and Colne and the centre of the town is an elegant mill in the eighteenth-century style with a pedimented façade. Shaw's mill in a steep valley below Stainland has late Victorian additions which turn it into a kind of Blenheim. The mill owner rebuilt his farmhouse beside the mill in a plain solid Regency style. From his front garden he could see the clock tower on the mill and judge whether his employees were punctual at work. Around the outlying mills, a farm is still to be found. Then came steam power. Mill owners were proud of its wonders. They installed steam-driven machinery. They built new mills on hilltops where there was more daylight. They added elegant chimneys to the old mills so that the prospect of Huddersfield is enhanced by these stately memorials of steam, though the white ashlar buildings of mills and houses have been blackened by them.

Before steam came, Huddersfield was already elegant. There are a chalybeate spring in a Grecian bathhouse and an hotel at Lockwood Spa. A local architect and engineer, Joseph Kaye, laid out a new Grecian town on the hilltop above the old church. He designed wide streets with two-storey houses, of clean cut stone. He was probably responsible for the elegant and now partially demolished Spring Street with its charming pedimented buildings at the top, built by public subscriptions in 1827 to house the first waterworks for the town. He also designed the Royal Infirmary in 1831 in the Doric style and St Paul's Church (1829) in the Gothic.

His portrait, with a mill in the background, is in the Art Gallery. He did for Huddersfield what John Nash did for London and we can probably ascribe to Kaye the layout for the streets in the centre of the town in the form of a grid with vistas down Ramsden Street, King Street and Princess Street to the open country and hills. The view down one of the chief streets, Kirkgate, has recently been blocked by a red and yellow eggbox in copybook contemporary for the YMCA. Kaye belonged to the times before professionalism, when engineers, architects and builders had less sharply defined functions.

Steam was crowned with glory at Huddersfield at the coming of the railways. The Lancashire and Yorkshire strode over from Penistone across the Holme Valley on the Lockwood viaduct (1847–8) of thirty-six stone arches. The London and North-Western on its way to Leeds joined with the Lancashire and Yorkshire in producing the most splendid station façade in England. It consists of a tall Corinthian central portico and long stone wings with smaller Corinthian porticoes at either end.

Joseph Kaye was the builder of this station in 1847–8, though J.P. Pritchett is given credit for the style. When it was completed it was suggested that Kaye's name and the date should be inscribed on the front but he said that the station itself would be the best record of its builder's name.

All that British Railways have done is to keep the façade dirty and caked with pigeon dung and quite needlessly to inscribe 'Huddersfield' on the frieze over the entrance portico as though one did not know one was in Huddersfield already.

The station forms one side of a grand classic square with the George Hotel on one side, the Huddersfield Building Society on the other and the Lion Building on the fourth. As the centre of an industrial town it could hardly be bettered.

Huddersfield had 7,000 inhabitants in 1801 and 10,000 by 1871. In religion it was largely Methodist. Nonconformists have favoured the classical style for their buildings and the Church of England and the Church of Rome preferred the Gothic. The most charming exteriors are the Nonconformists. The bold Highfield Congregational Church on New North Road is a baroque of 1843. Best of all is the Methodist Church in Queen Street, rebuilt in 1819 in Adam style in cut stone forming one side of a classic square.

The parish church of St Peter is a charming rebuilding of 1834 in the Perpendicular style with galleries, enamelled Georgian glass, painted churchwardens' staves and a golden east end by Sir Ninian Comper with his stained glass in the East Window. On the whole the churches are 'High' to counterbalance the Nonconformity. Old Huddersfield, to which the surrounding villages have come to market for the last 300 years, is a homely place of narrow alleys between the main straight streets, a Victorian covered market hall and a large Town Hall in the grand classic manner of the 1870s. Inside this a polished staircase leads to a life-size portrait of Queen Victoria. The hall itself, famed for its acoustics and concerts, has a splendid organ and case. The whole town is full of character and still full of 'brass'. There is a local daily, the *Huddersfield Examiner*, both excellent and old-established. We must forget the privy-less terrace houses, which survive here and there. We must hope for an imaginative replanning which will retain and repair the best of the older streets, such as Upper Spring Road and the streets off New North Road.

The mills are family concerns. Sykes, Crowther, Mallison, Taylor, Kenyon and Hoyle and Whitely are some of the famous names in worsted in Huddersfield which is reckoned to match the best worsted in the world. The way you can test a cloth is by how easily you can press your two thumbs through it. Huddersfield worsted is strongly resistant. So were the wool barons who made it. In Victorian times, greatly as they prospered, they did not leave their native towns. They left the old Georgian houses by the mill and built themselves big Victorian mansions on leafy heights north of the town at a suburb called Edgerton. It is the equivalent of Edgbaston in Birmingham, Broomhill in Sheffield and Headingley in Leeds. Winding roads under trees give glimpses down short drives flanked by laurel, of hidden riches beyond. You can walk down most of the drives now, because almost all the wool barons' houses have been turned into flats or institutions. Round the corner you see the mansion itself built of stone and heavily encrusted with decoration. One is Italianate, another gabled Gothic, a third Roman. Over the porch you may sometimes see carved the coat of arms purchased by the wool baron from the College of Heralds. The stained glass window in the staircased hall today no longer gives a mitigated light on antlers, grandfather clock, palms and the marble table with its polished silver salver for the cards of visitors. The panelled dining room no longer smells of roast beef and Yorkshire pudding after Sunday morning service in chapel or church. The lace curtains and watered silk have gone from the drawing room along with the Academy pictures of the seventies and eighties. Electricity has replaced gas. Partitions cut through cornices and plastic toys litter the overgrown garden. The houses have been converted into flats.

The last wool barons to live in state in their native town did not survive the thirties. Some, who were interested in art, employed that remarkable Art Nouveau architect of the North, Edgar Wood. He designed the strange clock tower in the suburb of Lindley and a large house, an Art Nouveau version of a Yorkshire manor house, called Banney Royd, in Edgerton. It is still there, empty, having been cruelly treated during the war by the National Fire Service. In Edgerton Cemetery below their houses, the wool barons lie, unequal even in death. Down the main drive are the famous names under obelisks and pillars. In other parts lie their clerks and managers under the lesser tombs, while the mill-hands are buried in cemeteries in other parts of the town. The descendants of the barons who still run their family businesses live away on the moors in Jaguar distance from their mills.

Huddersfield itself has been given to the people. The Corporation now owns most of the town. Not unnaturally the 'developers' have moved in and there are plans afoot for destroying most of the old centre of the town, including the work of Kaye, such as the Infirmary and Spring Street. There are even plans to destroy the famous Methodist chapel and its square. The little alleys with their individual shops, to which people have gone for generations, are to go.

The brutal façade of the new branch of Boots in King Street is an earnest of what is to come. So are the Co-op and the new Civic Centre, Technical College and chain stores.

Some will say that this new hygienic, washable and packaged world of the housewife is preferable to the old slums and palaces of inequality. Others will regret the passing of a town of great character and Georgian and Victorian beauty into a replica of Slough or the Middle West of America. Before it is too late we must hope that the hand of the 'developer' will be stayed and that the centre at least of Huddersfield and the well laid out Georgian streets will be restored by internal reconstruction and an outside wash.

***

Brighton: Old Ocean's Bauble

6 November 1964

৪৩⅁ঙ

The train service from the metropolis is fast and frequent. It is also bumpy and you cannot read. Instead, a walk down the corridors gives a foretaste of the place. Some Pullmans decorated with inlaid mahogany and silvered fittings in a delightful Adam style recall good King Edward VII. In them sit the famous stage people who live in Brighton, and pleasure-loving peers and rich company inflators. Other Pullmans are veneered in cubist patterns of the late 1920s. Here sit stage people on their way up and those whose shares are going down. A few solitaries try to read prospectuses and administration charts in the Firsts of the ordinary Southern rolling stock. Holiday-makers, children and regular commuters fill the rocking Seconds. Each section has its pale invalids — a wife wrapped up in rugs beside her husband, a husband with his sticks with rubber tips. We slide by the grey slate roofs of Preston, the red brick Noah's Ark of St Bartholomew's rises from the little houses near the station, and here is the great roofed terminus, and the station house itself of the early 1840s, designed by Sir John Rennie, who engineered the tunnels through the Downs in 1841. As we alight at this elevated terminus above the town, we smell the sea, despite the fumes of diesel. Here, for more than a century, millions of travellers by rail from London have smelt the sea before us.

In *Brighton* Osbert Sitwell quotes Li Shu-Ch'ang, the secretary to the first Chinese Ambassador in London, who visited Brighton in 1877: 'Since then, years have passed and I have visited famous places in many lands; but never on any day has Pu-lai-tun (Brighton) been absent from my thoughts, such power does this place hold over the affections of all who have beheld it.' Let us step down into the town and see if what he says still holds true.

The demolition men and 'developers' have moved in. The local authorities have put up well-intentioned slabs and cubes whose outline, materials and texture are un-Brighton and look back to the priggery of the thirties though they have been built in the sixties. Still, much of the town is left; the noble stucco terraces swaggering in a light reflected from the English Channel have verandahs of delicate ironwork, bow windows, with lawns and flowers below them. Brighton and Hove between them (the Peace Memorial on the front marks the division of the boroughs) are still the best looking seaside town in Britain.

So they will remain, provided they keep their joyful Georgian and Victorian character. The Brighton Corporation seems aware of this.

The town welcomes you. Every lamp post that can be festooned with coloured electric light bulbs along the front and main streets is so adorned. Fountains, statues and trees are floodlit. More floodlit, more begardened and more fantastic than all, down in the very centre, rise the domes and minarets of George IV's Marine Palace, the Royal Pavilion. 'What we see today is a gradual accretion,' says Sir John Summerson, 'and to attempt to judge the building as a unity is to miss the point of it ... the Pavilion is on the plane of a book written by somebody for his own amusement over a long period.'

The Prince's architect, charged with converting a staid, late eighteenth-century villa by Henry Holland into the present oriental palace, was John Nash, who started work on it, for about ten years, in 1815. This building, so much despised by our grandparents for its extravagance and artificiality, was bought with incredible foresight by the town from Queen Victoria, together with ample land around it, for £50,000 in 1850, when 'developers' were already threatening the site. Now the Pavilion, outside and in, has been sensitively restored to its Eastern splendour. It is the spirit of pleasure-loving, anti-puritan Brighton, but it is not the origin of the town.

Brighton, once Brighthelmstone, was a mediaeval fishing port of some size, with gates and walls. It was important enough to be invaded by the French in 1514. Later, it supplied London with fish, being the nearest Channel fishing port on the coast. Walls of

Sussex flint and old brick and red-tiled roofs survive in The Lanes, where the antique shops are, and have a fishing town look. Bathing in the sea for pleasure started at Scarborough in about 1730 and less than ten years later was practised at Brighton. Until then, genteel people considered the sea ugly and dangerous.

It was on a visit there in 1783 that the Prince fell in love with Brighton. He liked its treeless, chalky landscape and the thunder of its shingly beach. Brighton became fashionable. Houses were built, first as near as their builders dared to the Royal Pavilion, then along the cliffs. With unparalleled imagination and courage, an architect, C.A. Busby (1788–1834), a local builder-architect, Amon Wilds (c. 1762–1833), and Wilds's son, Henry, laid out stucco houses along the front, in the manner of John Nash in Regent Street and Regent's Park in London. But their houses were even taller and grander, and were ingeniously adapted to sloping sites. Among the terraces facing the sea, they put squares and crescents.

The grandest of these are Lewes Crescent and Sussex Square in Kemptown laid out (1823–8) by Busby and Wilds on land owned by an MP called Kemp. The next grandest scheme is Brunswick Place in Hove (1824–30). The remarkable Park Crescent, hidden from the sea, with its winding gardens, was designed by Henry Wilds in 1829. The great Sir Charles Barry, from London, designed a new church in the Gothic style in the centre of the town, north of the Steine. Hypochondriacs are usually interested in religion. Proprietary chapels for popular preachers and other chapels for Nonconformists were built in the cheerful, stucco streets and squares. As many people as could afford to come to Brighton by coach, did so.

Then the town had a lean time. George IV and his brother William died, and the town had overbuilt itself. Queen Victoria and Prince Albert didn't like the place: too many trippers looked in through the Pavilion windows. Brighton was saved by the railways. They came by the shortest route from London (47½ miles) in 1840; in that year also a line was built round to Hove and six years later another line to Lewes. Immense and splendid viaducts of Sussex brick were built to carry the rails, the finest being that on the Kemptown branch (1869) which is now closed. London flocked to the sea. All available space was filled in with little houses. The hotel servants, shop assistants, bathing machine attendants, railwaymen and those who could afford only cheap lodgings lived in little bay-windowed houses, flimsy three-storey imitations of their grand originators on the front. The steep combes which meet at the Steine had slopes of blue slate roof instead of turf.

The sea was for pleasure, the hills for worship. Two piers were built. The old chain pier of 1823 was used as a promenade for invalids and, in 1836, steam packets called there for a new route to France via Dieppe, though this was eclipsed by the Newhaven route ten years later, where landing was safer. The chain pier was blown away in 1896 and the present Palace Pier is as new as 1901. The West Pier (1866) is now the older.

Victorian Brighton looked towards the poorer people inland among the hills and built churches. Two Victorian Brighton vicars, father and son, named Wagner, were scandalised at the way servants were not allowed to attend churches where their masters and mistresses worshipped and at the high prices charged for pews. The son, the famous Father Wagner, was rich. He built splendid Gothic churches in the poorer parts of the town. Thus it is that Brighton is rivalled only by Leeds in magnificent churches of the Church of England. St Bartholomew's (1874) is the tallest church in England. St Martin's (1875), St Mary Kemptown (1877) and St Michael (1858–93) are equally magnificent. St Paul (1848), lone among amusement arcades and demolitions of West Street, was the start of this High Church mission to Brighton, which came to be known as 'London, Brighton and South Coast religion'.

You can see what happened later. The buildings tell you. The middle classes were growing and wanted separate houses with gardens of their own. This was the chance for the rival town of Hove which became a borough in 1898. Already Victorian houses in brick, considered more honest than false stucco, were appearing beyond Adelaide Crescent. Even the schools were leaving Brighton. It was too plebeian. Roedean left Lewes Crescent in 1896. Red terracotta blocks of flats and Tudor, tile-hung villas sprawled inland over the Downs. Hove thought of itself as a sort of Westgate-on-Sea to Brighton's Margate. The motor-car age suited Hove. There was more room for the garage. Brighton tried out terracotta too, to vie with its rival, and the Metropole was built in 1890 by Alfred Waterhouse on the front.

By now the tide has turned. Hove sinks as Brighton rises. Georgian has come in fashion and Kemptown, long neglected, is the smartest part. Stucco is at a premium. Brick and terracotta are out. Unfortunately, there has been, and continues to be, wretched 'judicious infilling' by speculators in Georgian Brighton and Victorian Hove. It is in the form of dull cubes and slabs of flats. The rot started in the thirties, when Embassy Court was built against a Georgian terrace on the front. This was done on the serious and misguided theory that if a building is the expression of its age, it will look well alongside the expression of a former age. As it is of different proportions and with horizontal lines instead of vertical and of only slightly different texture, it only looks as though the owners were getting in as much rent as possible for as many floors as they could cram into its awkward shape.

Much worse has been done in Hove. And in Brighton itself the top of the Metropole has been shaved of its old skyline, and given clumsy glass penthouses. The whole area of commercial Brighton between the two piers is to be demolished. Except for the Grand Hotel (1864), The Lanes and a few early buildings, it was never much. What will it be like now the 'developers' are in? If they encroach any more into the Georgian and Victorian, they will have ruined the town architecturally, historically and, what matters to the 'developers', commercially. We will all have to go to Ramsgate, Folkestone, Margate, Dover and Southend.

Winter:
When Southend Finds Charm

12 February 1965

೫)೦ଓ

To many London children Southend is their first sight of the sea. Charlie Chaplin, in his autobiography, gives a lyrical and moving description of his childhood visit to it with his mother and elder brother, Sidney. They were at their very poorest and suddenly had enough money for a day trip to Southend. He describes the steep down-slope from the station, the amazing wall of water at the bottom of the slope, the golden sand and coloured buckets and balloons. It was Paradise.

But for us sophisticated town explorers, older than Charlie Chaplin was then, winter is the time to see it. Winter in midweek with a strong wind whipping up the broad waters of the Thames mouth and the great ships anchored off the Nore, waiting to enter the Port of London, visibly rocking although they are a mile or more out to sea: winter, when the horrible smell of fish and chips frying for the summer visitors has left the front and the salt sea breeze returns strong and wonderful as wine: winter, when the Kursaal is shut and there is rust on the rails of the mountain railways, and huge plastic Walt Disney figures lie prone in sheds or strapped under flapping awnings: winter, when the snug little inland bungalows of this town of 170,000 residents let out their shoppers into the afternoon streets. Winter is the time to see Southend. It is a new, invigorating capital, not an hour from London.

No one in his senses would make the journey there by road; it is a hellish experience from London, because of traffic to the docks. Nor is the longer journey by Great Eastern from Liverpool Street so interesting as the thirty-five-mile run from Fenchurch Street on the London, Tilbury and Southend line. I like to catch the noon train on, say, a Tuesday in March when this well-worn, hidden City terminus of brick and iron is almost deserted. We pull out on arches above the East End chimney pots and see the great, white, limestone steeples of Hawksmoor's east London churches – Christ Church, Spitalfields, St George's-in-the-East and St Anne Limehouse – sailing like galleons under the clouds.

Then we look down into a deserted cemetery as big as a fair-sized park, all elders and undergrowth and toppled-over gravestones. A white wooden windmill dominates Upminster, where we say goodbye to the London Underground system and hurtle over the Essex marshes. This is real country, surely the nearest real country to London, with timbered and plastered farms, wooden barns with red tiles on their roofs, wide flat fields and a distant view to the south across the marshes to the broadening Thames and the far-off Kentish hills. Inland are elmy heights and flint and brick country churches.

Suddenly, a grim reminder of the do-goodery of modern planners, we race through the New Town of Basildon, which has no station here. Winds sweep over its exposed shopping centre and watery car parks. Rain washes the modernistic mosaic fascia above a shopping arcade, intended, no doubt, to strike a 'gay' note, but now a little out of date in its abstract design. Then there is more real country and the old village of Benfleet climbs the slope around its silvery church tower. Here a bridge crosses to flat Canvey Island and the landscape is three-quarters sky. Now we race through the pleasantest scenery of all: on the south bank, a creek full of small boats, on the left a grassy cliff with wooded slopes kept as a nature reserve. At the highest point stand the ruined curtain walls of Hadleigh Castle, as romantic from the train as in Constable's famous picture.

Then we come to a halt at Leigh-on-Sea, the eastern limit of the Borough of Southend. We glide slowly past the row of wooden cockle sheds and the flaps of one of them may be open with steam coming out where they are steaming the cockles.

Leigh High Street is like something in Dickens, with hipped roofs and weather-boarded houses among the brown brick. Now Southend gets more like Metroland, with little villas of 1920 Tudor and 1930 Moderne among lovingly tended private gardens of shrubs, crazy-paving and bird-baths. At Westcliff-on-Sea it becomes like West Hampstead with Edwardian red-brick hotels and terraces, gabled and turreted.

Here is the Southend Central Station. We cross to the lofty 1860 booking hall as big as a ballroom, and so out into the town. This is the High Street Charlie Chaplin saw sloping down to the sea. It is a bit of a disappointment now, with all the usual chain stores, and might as well be Hounslow or West Bromwich. Here at the bottom on the right a charming late Georgian hotel and terrace, verandahed and of yellow brick and stucco, looks over wind-slashed ornamental shrubs to the faintly seen Isle of Sheppey and mouth of the Medway. Below us, the pier, the longest pleasure pier in Europe, runs a mile and a third over mud or water according to the state of the tide. We get in the electric train and, in an hour from London, we are lunching in the friendly, warm, municipal restaurant on the Pier head with the water rolling round us, and looking out at the wide North Sea and the waiting ships. It is the greatest change in the shortest time that London has to offer.

Sitting here and looking inland along the whole six miles of sea front which compose modern Southend, we can picture the growth of the place. First a grassy incline in the estuary with a twelfth-century Benedictine priory built at Prittlewell of flint and stone, and later a church for the village above it. Then the rich arable land in the seventeenth-century caused yeoman farmers to prosper and Dutch-looking manor houses were built of red brick and timber here and there, of which the finest survival is Porters at Southchurch, now the parlour of the Lord Mayor, and quite near the large cob-and-thatch village of Prittlewell. Further inland, up the Thames was, and still is, Leigh, with its fifteenth-century church tower above the brick and wooden fishing village which once sent ships to the Armada.

In late Georgian times, sea-bathing became the vogue and the people of Essex came to stay in boarding houses at the south end of the parish of Prittlewell. Some houses were built along what is now Marine Parade, and they have become cafés and amusement arcades, and the elegant Royal Terrace was built on the cliffs. In 1830 a pier was started for steamers from London. Always, the deadly rival of the Essex coast was Kent with Herne Bay and Margate. To compete, the pier was extended several times until by 1949 it was pushed out to the full length it is now and the railway carried more than 4½ million passengers. Let us look at this long stretch of pier before seeing more of Southend. At high or low tide, it is the best place in Britain for ship spotters. More than 50,000 ships of over 100 tons pass it each year: Union Castle, Ellerman, Cunarders, tankers, and local traders, and at low tide there are the bawleys on the sandy mud. Flounders, dab, herring, bass, garfish, plaice, whiting and eels may be caught at different places along the pier.

In 1856 the railway came from Fenchurch Street and that was the beginning of the renewed seaside resort. By good King Edward's reign, there was a rush and Westcliff was founded between Leigh and the Georgian terrace at the south end of Prittlewell. It was the smartest and richest part and was to Southend what Hove was to Brighton. In the mid-wars period, all gaps were filled up with villas at Thorpe Bay and Chalkwell. And, of course, with all this development went new churches, most of them High Anglican. The most prominent, rising like a battleship made of yellow brick above the two-storey houses and Kursaal seen from the pier, is St Erkenwald's, by Sir Walter Tapper (1905) and still incomplete. The most beautiful is St Alban, Westcliff, by Sir Charles Nicholson, a Southend man, built 1898–1908, with a perfect, many vistaed Arts and Crafts interior, brightly painted – Heals gone Anglican.

So much of Southend is sky and cloud formation, sunset and storm and constantly changing light, that, as we walk back along the pier, drinking air, we are one with the elements and forget that we ever knew London.

Ever knew London? Alas, on the long walk back inland along the pier, a monstrous 'developer's' slab confronts us, and others are rising. Southend is trying to imitate London, ceasing to be itself and becoming the international nothingness which goes with those who put money before aesthetics and profits before local character. The fish bars, where delicious fresh cockles, mussels, shrimps, oysters and prawns may be bought, are dwarfed by menacing rent-collecting slabs of the packaged age of the housewife, and soon, unless the enlightened Borough Council can call a halt to it, or Mr George Brown calls a halt, the sunny Southend of Charlie Chaplin and pleasure will be no more.

Before we leave for London and barbarism, let us visit the Beecroft Art Gallery on Westcliff Parade. Here are pictures of Georgian, Victorian and Edwardian Southend and Leigh, here are memories of the great part the sailors and fishermen on this Essex bank played in the last war. Here are fine paintings by Constable, Harpigny and Edward Bawden. Then, with the strong air nearly sending us to sleep, let us hurtle back to Fenchurch Street, the other way on from the commuters.

***

Palaces from Pills

19 March 1965

ঙ০ cჳ

Hidden among Surrey conifers and birches are two of the most amazing buildings in Britain. They are the result of the munificence of a patent medicine vendor, Mr Thomas Holloway (1800–1883), and the genius of his architect, Mr William Henry Crossland (1834–1909), a pupil of Sir Gilbert Scott. The two buildings are within a few miles of each other – the Holloway

Sanatorium (1871–85), Virginia Water, and the Royal Holloway College (1883–6), Egham.

They have to be seen to be believed, and once seen they haunt the mind like a recurring and exalting dream. The Sanatorium is enormous domestic Gothic in red brick and white Portland stone with towers, turrets and gables outside, and painted staircases and halls within. The College is also of red brick and Portland stone, but in French Renaissance style, recalling Chambord and Blois.

Thomas Holloway was born in Devonport. His father had been a warrant officer in the Navy in the wars against Napoleon, and then set up as a baker. The family moved to Cornwall and Thomas was educated in Camborne and Penzance, in which his now widowed mother and his brother ran a grocer's shop. He moved to London in 1828 to seek his fortune and spent some years in France, before setting up in London as a merchant and agent. He bought a patent ointment from an Italian, which was made of harmless herbs, and persuaded the senior surgeon of the Middlesex Hospital to recommend it. In 1837 he advertised it in all the leading papers and was, indeed, the first exponent of extensive and attractive advertising. He was also its first martyr, because he bought more space in the newspapers than he could afford and was put into Whitecross Street Prison for debt.

When he came out, he was able to pay his creditors in full with an added 10 per cent for their trouble. In 1840 he married Jane Driver, the daughter of a Rotherhithe shipwright, and started making laxative pills, largely of castor oil and ginger. He and his wife worked from four in the morning till ten at night, and Holloway used to take his pills down to the docks and sell them to those taking long sea voyages as a remedy against constipation and skin trouble from the food on sailing ships. He then took up advertising in a still bigger way and had his advertisements translated into every language under the sun.

The French only would not sell his medicines. He and his wife lived frugally over their shop which was eventually moved to New

Oxford Street. His advertising account, which was £5,000 in 1842, rose to £50,000 per annum at the end of his life and his ledgers show that his annual profit was about the same amount. His portraits show a handsome, clean-shaven man with firm chin and dark brown eyes, and wide, determined mouth. He was a shrewd speculator and so increased his fortune that by 1870 he was a considerable Surrey landowner. For instance, when there was a delay in getting bricks for his Sanatorium, he bought up a brick works and sold the products to his builders. He supervised every financial detail of his two institutions and used his brother-in-law, George Martin-Holloway, as his agent. He was a philanthropist of foresight. He first offered a large gift of money to his native town, which refused it.

Then Lord Shaftesbury pointed out to him that, whereas there were large lunatic asylums for the poor, and very dismal Victorian places they were, and, whereas there were more sumptuous homes for the rich insane, like The Retreat, York (1795), there was no place for the insane of the professional middle classes: lawyers, doctors, clergymen and servicemen. For lawyers, doctors and priests Holloway had contempt. Yet he and his brother-in-law visited mental hospitals in England and America, and pooled their experience in the design for the Sanatorium for such people. They decided that each patient should have his own room; that the public rooms should be cheerful, sumptuous and full of decoration. Hence the amazing halls and staircase at Virginia Water. So advanced was Holloway's plan that Dr Roderick Macdonald, its present Physician Superintendent, was able to say that Holloway 'formulated concepts of the care and treatment of mentally ill people nearly a century ahead of current thought and which, in fact, have only become commonplace in this country in the second quarter of this century'.

Holloway gave £300,000 towards the building of his Sanatorium. The College was an equally far-sighted undertaking for the education of women, who in those days had little chance of getting to the older universities. Holloway appointed governors from the Corporation of London and the University of London and gave £400,000 and the site. The chapel was to be interdenominational.

Art was introduced inside the building in the form of a picture gallery. He paid over £32,000 for well-known works by such men as Frith, Landseer, Millais and Copley Fielding, who are just coming into their own again after nearly a century of unpopularity. In all, this rugged individualist gave a million pounds in charity, which would be worth £20 million today. He is buried under a sombre classic tomb of red granite in Sunninghill churchyard. Someone should write his life history, for there are still pungent stories about him in his institutions and there must somewhere be letters, papers and accounts.

Holloway's architect, Crossland, seems to have been a likeable, exuberant person, but exactly where and when he was born and where and when he died, and whether he married and had children, I cannot discover.

He was not a rigid Gothicist even at the height of the Gothic revival. He went in for the competition for the Sanatorium in 1871. 'I did not feel inclined to go single-handed into this competition,' he wrote in 1887, 'and I sought the assistance of the late John Philpott Jones, in whose hands I practically left the working out of the design. When the adjudicating was given in our favour, I was up in the woods of Nova Scotia, thinking a good deal more of salmon and moose than sanatoria. One day, however, I was recalled to my duties by a telegram from Mr Jones, to say that we were the winners of the competition, and that I had better come home, which I did very reluctantly.' Jones died and Holloway was on the site every day. He was extremely annoyed to find that ornamental bricks were working out at 2d. and 3d. each, so Crossland suggested Portland stone instead of bricks for the dressings.

When the building was finished, Holloway turned his mind to building a college for women which became a memorial to his wife.

'"Will you do this, Mr Crossland?" To which I answered most assuredly I would. He then patted me on the shoulder, and said: "My boy, you shall have the work; but mind, on the condition that you sketch and measure Chambord from bottom to top. No more competitions for me. I had too much trouble about the last."'

So Crossland went, and measured many chateaux including Chambord where Holloway joined him. Crossland thought that there had been enough revived Gothic and, despite the efforts of 'highly educated ladies' to persuade Holloway to build a Gothic college, Crossland prevailed. His plan is vast and clear. It is a double quadrangle 500 feet from east to west and 350 feet from north to south. The longer blocks were built to contain sitting rooms and bedrooms for each student and a common room for every six of the 350 students housed.

Fortunately, the interior furnishings have been little disturbed, and the elaborate interdenominational chapel is just as Crossland left it, a late Victorian masterpiece, with gilded ironwork, ivory coloured reliefs on the sculptured ceiling, hanging lamps, carved stalls of dark wood and painted walls, all in a Renaissance style that was Crossland's own.

Crossland seems thoroughly to have enjoyed himself during the four and a half years he lived on the site. 'The Mount Lee Estate was placed at my disposal, and I had Windsor Forest for exercise ground. The setting-out shed and the sculptors' studio were my delight; and altogether I found myself leading a life we architects read about but few experience.'

Holloway trusted Crossland and only visited the College site four times. 'He never, or perhaps very seldom, praised anyone. There was, however, one exception; when, on his third visit to the College after its completion, he once again, after six years, patted me on the back and said: "*Well done*, Mr Crossland, I am more than pleased."'

And so will you be who visit the College today, which is as sound structurally as when it was built, and where you may see the Academy masterpieces in the art gallery, which Holloway gave and which have been as long out of fashion as Crossland's architecture.

***

Belongs to Glasgow

7 May 1965

ဆုင္သ

 is not generally remembered that Oscar Wilde, besides being famous as a playwright, talker and poet, was a leading authority on decoration. His ideas and sense of colour were much in advance of his time. He was a friend of such controversial figures in the world of art as Whistler, who had been influenced by the then unknown art of Japan, and who brought a libel action in 1877 against Ruskin for condemning his *Nocturne in Black and Gold* – a painting of a falling rocket. I love Whistler, with his appreciation of mist and smoke and fog and pale colours and white and gold, and how Oscar Fingal O'Flahertie Wills Wilde came to be associated with the New Art and the Celtic knots, which deliciously intertwine to make the initial word of this article, is an interesting story. These initial letters were drawn by Archibald Knox (1864–1933), the Manx artist who designed for Libertys. The poet Yeats also liked Celtic knots and the New Art (or *l'Art Nouveau*, as it was called in France, *Jugendstil* in Germany) and the covers of his books of poems had designs in this manner by T. Sturge Moore. Words like mystic, faerie, quaint, ancient and, of course, artistic, are

associated with the Celtic twilight, which was the mother of the New Art, whose father was Glasgow.

To understand how this came about, you will have to look at Glasgow, the second city of the great and growing British Empire as it was in the 1880s. James Watt had walked on Glasgow Green in 1764 and first thought of how to make his steam engine work. Steam drove the Glasgow cotton mills. Coal was mined round the city and steam tugs and steam boats were built in the shipyards of the Clyde. Marine engineering brought fortunes to the inventive citizens of this ancient merchant city. Around the grimly impressive mediaeval Cathedral of St Mungo, whose interior is one of the finest Gothic buildings of Europe, rose the hundred spires of kirks belonging to the manifold forms of Scottish Presbyterianism. Against a rainy sky, a hill called the Necropolis near the cathedral bristles with the obelisks, broken columns and urns of departed ironmasters, coal owners, marine engineers.

At one time men of this sort lived in the handsome Greek Revival terraces and crescents of the western parts of the town, which rival the New Town of Edinburgh in their sterner majesty. Out of a park laid out by Paxton rises a hill crowned with the fairy-like Gothic outline of Sir Gilbert Scott's Glasgow University, to which they sent their sons. The kirks, the banks, the domes, the railways rumbling in over arches to Buchanan Street, Queen Street, St Enoch and Central, this was where the New Art was born. Here and there survived bits of mediaeval and eighteenth-century Glasgow. Here too, down narrow closes, were the most terrible slums of Britain, many of which are still there.

Glasgow is a self-sufficient place where money is thought more of than breeding and where, if a man can make his way, he is honoured whatever his origin. From the Middle Ages, Glasgow has been a city of trade guilds and merchants. In the last century it owed its prosperity largely to marine engineering and its eyes were turned westward. The Clyde and the open sea mattered more than the rest of Scotland and England. Its citizens loved it, and neither were they indifferent to painting and architecture. They never had been, from the days when the cathedral was built. In the last century Glasgow was the first city to appreciate and collect French impressionists. It may be safely said that the best and most representative provincial gallery of paintings from Italian primitives to the present day is the Glasgow Art Gallery, and this has been assembled and paid for by its citizens.

The rumours of Whistler and Wilde's white rooms in Chelsea had reached Glasgow in the eighties. Sir John Lavery, James Guthrie, W.Y. Macgregor, Joseph Crawhall, D.Y. Cameron and E.A. Walton are still famous names as members of what was called the Glasgow School. It was the youngest brother of the last named, George Walton, born in Glasgow in 1867, who may be described as the founder of the New Art style. 'I began in Glasgow in 1888,' he wrote to me, 'and was working among the founders of the Glasgow School of Painters. The architectural work was influenced considerably by Whistler. His exhibitions were being held in London about this time and, in arrangement and colour, were the most remarkable events of the time, and brought a gaiety into all contemporary decoration by the use of white paint and simple light colours on walls etc.' George Walton, a tall, gentle, quiet man, handsome, clean-shaven and with high Scottish cheekbones, was a Glasgow bank clerk and the son of a painter whose family had known prosperity. In 1888 he set up in Glasgow as an interior decorator, and never lacked for work until the Great War of 1914. He built as well as decorated, and there survives at Shiplake a house he designed in 1908 which looks like a Regency Thames barge painted white and come to rest in a meadow. The verandahed wall on its river side is almost entirely of glass. Walton, like all the architects of his time who were not commercial go-getters, designed not just the house, but everything in it; door handles, furniture, fabrics, carpets and stained glass. Living in the Glasgow of the eighties, he would have despised the Greek and Roman Revival architecture of the substantial Victorian houses, banks, warehouses and kirks of the city; he would have thought them dead imitations of a past time. Equally, he would have despised the revival of English Gothic by Sir Gilbert Scott in the new buildings of the University. He was a Scot, and went for his inspiration to the old Scots buildings with no conscious style about them: farmhouses, fishermen's cottages and crofts.

Of Charles Rennie Mackintosh much has been written. He was the son of a Glasgow police superintendent and in 1889 joined the Glasgow firm of architects Honeyman and Keppie. He and Walton had much in common, though Walton was the older by a year, and Mackintosh used to sketch the old Scottish castles. The influence of Whistler, and later of Aubrey Beardsley, was strong upon them and Mackintosh, with his beautiful draughtsmanship, produced drawings of buildings which were a kind of Aubrey Beardsley version of the stern Scottish baronial. They were tall and thin and the lines of construction were emphasised. He delighted, as did George Walton, in simplicity.

Walton and Mackintosh were founders of New Art. But there is the decorative side too. At the Glasgow Art School, conducted by Francis H. Newbery — Fra Newbery as he was called — were many handsome, high-cheekboned girl students with freckles and wide-apart grey eyes. They admired the rough harled houses that the menfolk thought so fine and Scottish, but there was also the fey mysterious side of Scotland too, the wee folk in the hills and Oisin, son of Finn Mac Cumhail, and the ancient Celtic kings and queens and the Celtic saints. Did not they like finely woven cramoisy silk and plaids, and could not their legends be depicted in stained glass and mural paintings after the manner of Aubrey Beardsley himself and the great James McNeill Whistler, who had been given an honorary degree by Glasgow University? Aye, they could, and they were. Miss Cranston's teashops in Glasgow, where many a bap and bannock were eaten, were decorated by Walton and Mackintosh and Margaret, the wife of Mackintosh, in this delicate, simple style of pale Whistlerish colours, Aubrey Beardsley wi' a Scots accent. And very nice and delicate it was, and highly original, and not sham eighteenth century at all.

Walton became well known in England for his decoration of the Kodak shops and the word Kodak on the film packets still faintly recalls the Glasgow New Art style. Neither Mackintosh nor Walton was good at business and they died poor. They would have been very surprised had they lived into our own day, to find themselves heralded by 'art historians' as the pioneers of modern architecture. They were artists and architects who admired simplicity of construction, and who had the innate sense of proportion of all great architects. Their work was reproduced in *The Studio* from 1893 onwards and this monthly magazine of art and architecture had more influence in Europe and America than any other until 1914. Julius Hoffman built in Brussels and Austria handsome, simple houses in the Walton and Mackintosh style. In France, the simplicity became twisted like water lily roots. In Germany it was brutalised into squares and cubes which have come back to us in the form of Odeons. Only here and there, where a real artist got hold of it, like Baillie Scott, the architect, and Sir Alfred Gilbert, and Reynolds Stephens, the sculptor, the metalworkers Bainbridge Reynolds, Harry Wilson and Archibald Knox, did it really come into its own. It is too romantic, delicate and personal to have anything to do with what is considered new today.

***

Are These Britain's Most Unregarded Buildings?

6 August 1965

ಬಃಿ

Customs Houses as architecture have never had the consideration and illustration they deserve. Perhaps we shy off them as we do from police stations and County Courts, because we fear arrest or a fine. Yet, looking at them in moments of disinterestedness and comparative innocence, I have been amazed at the variety of their architecture. They are often splendid or charming buildings and in the most unexpected places. At Peterborough, on the river bank, and dwarfed by the ill-placed electric power station which ruins that city, is a small and elegant early Renaissance, seventeenth- or early eighteenth-century limestone building, once the Custom House and now, since Peterborough has declined as a seaport, the headquarters of a local organisation.

The richness and variety of Custom House architecture led me to the London headquarters of the department. These are no longer in the Custom House on the Thames (D. Laing 1813–17, rebuilt R. Smirke 1825–6), which is confined to HM Customs' work in the Port of London, but in a formidably dull and ugly modern building of the thirties called King's Beam House, near Tower Hill Underground Station. In this uninspiring place, the Customs & Excise services have carved out for themselves a sort of regimental headquarters, a living memorial to their long traditions. There are a library with a librarian, a museum, a board room with portraits and painted coats of arms, and a private suite for the top Commissioners of Customs & Excise, full of prints, showcases and handsome eighteenth-century and Regency furniture.

Custom duties are what we pay to the government on goods coming in from abroad. Excise duties are paid on home-produced goods on which the government decides to levy a tax, e.g. whisky and gin. In 1909 they were amalgamated into the single department now known as HM Customs & Excise.

One has the sense that this compact, little-known and comparatively small service is a friendly regiment, whose officers and men are all known to each other. Moreover, the work cannot, at any rate in the past, have been so exacting as to make its members miserable and non-creative. From the list of well-known men who have been in the Customs & Excise services, I found displayed the names of Chaucer, Congreve, Matthew Prior, Daniel Defoe, Nicholas Rowe, John Newton, Captain Marryat, Robert Burns, Horace Walpole (who was Clerk of the Pipe, whatever that delightful sinecure may have been), Tom Paine and William Allingham. Our own poet, Richard Church, once worked in the London Custom House.

The Customs service that we know today was founded by Charles II in 1671, who appointed a Board of Commissioners; today the Board of Customs & Excise is still appointed under Royal Warrant. Under them, the country is divided into thirty-five 'Collections', with a Collector in charge of each, who now looks after both Customs and Excise. There are three sorts of Customs officials. The most numerous and least known are plain-clothes men who examine imported and exported goods and see that the duties are paid on them. They work at seaports and airports and in the towns all over the kingdom. Next come the uniformed preventive officers who are known as the Waterguards — even if they are working at airports — the only members of the service well known to the public. Their duty is to prevent smuggling. Thirdly are the indoor officers who work in the Collectors' offices behind the counter.

To those who read the history of Customs men, the smugglers whom they have intercepted are not so romantic as fiction makes them. In the lean times after the Napoleonic Wars, smuggling had become a profession and the preventive officers, together with the armed forces, were at war with smugglers all along our coasts. During this war, and after it, they built up the life-saving services, the lighthouse and lightship and coastguard services. Today there are still three revenue cruisers, HMRC *Venturous*, *Vincent* and *Valiant*, flying the portcullis flag of the service.

There are still curious old terms in the service. 'Rummaging' a ship is the work of the preventive officers when searching a ship for contraband. The official who sits at the west end of the Long Room in the London Custom House is called the Bench Clerk. The chief office in a Custom House, where the skippers or their agents report, is always called the Long Room, whatever its shape. This is said to date from when Wren built the London Custom House on the site of the present one in 1669. He made the chief room in the building on the first floor overlooking the river and wrote on his plan 'the Long Room'. The name has stuck, and many Custom Houses throughout the world have their Long Room.

The larger Custom Houses were built on a plan which made the Long Room the focal point. This was generally on the first floor and approached by an imposing staircase. In the seventeenth and early eighteenth centuries, when the Palladian style came in, the approach to the Long Room was by an external staircase, as at Poole. The first Custom Houses of Charles II's time and later were intended to emphasise loyalty to the monarch in the building where dues to him were paid. They were something more than the Town Hall. They were waterside royal buildings on the quay. Even the smaller Custom Houses made a great display of the Royal Arms, as at Boston (Lincs) and Fowey.

From 1820 till 1850, when many large Custom Houses were built, they continued in the classic style – I do not think there is such a thing in the United Kingdom as a Gothic Revival Custom House – but they were less royal looking and more governmental. In England, the brothers Robert and Sydney Smirke, who collared so many official jobs through being safe, unoriginal men 'in with Government', rebuilt in the Ionic Greek style the London Custom House. Scottish architects, who were at this time bolder designers in the Greek and Roman styles than the English, put up some fine Custom Houses, notably at Greenock and Leith. Today, if the new Custom House at Hull is typical, the style is even more anonymous – just semi-permanent sheds and brick and glass, giving no sense of the great tradition and history of the service. One cannot, unfortunately, hope much from the architecture of Custom Houses at airports either.

***

The Isle of Man

29 October 1965

&DCB

There are white horses all over the sea below us, which make me glad I came by air. And here is the island in the Irish Sea. Scotland, Wales and the Mountains of Mourne can all be seen on a clear day from the highest mountain peak, Snaefell (2,034 feet), in the middle. The Isle of Man is thirty-three miles long and twelve miles wide, much more mountainous, wooded, varied and countrified than the travel posters would have us believe.

At Ronaldsway Airport, we are in a foreign country. The flag of the island, three legs on a red background, flaps over us. The money is different, there are Manx pound and ten shilling notes. The stamps are different; much prettier than ours in England, and the Queen on them is not the Queen, but Lord of Man. Income tax is different too, if you are one of the 50,000 inhabitants, three-quarters of whom are native Manx, a mixture of Norse and Celtic stock. The rest are what are locally called 'come-overs', or 'when-Is' ('When I was in Baluchistan'), who have wisely chosen this beautiful friendly place for their declining years and inadequate pensions. Above all, the light is different, and very different, from the grey, cold of Manchester Airport, which we left half an hour ago. Today it is sparkling and clear and the water in it magnifies colours. The sun, reflected from the sea, brings up the grass to emerald and makes granite, limestone, slate and red sandstone shine like jewels and the flowers are brighter still. The air is different too, warmer and gentler than in Manchester, because we are in the Gulf Stream, and over there, beside the airfield, is the outline of King William's College, with its tower and handsome Georgian Gothic castellations. It is the school about which Dean Farrar wrote his famous novel *Eric, or Little by Little*.

And now, we will go by road to Douglas, past hedges and farms and stone-built cottages which seem rather like Cornwall, until enclosing ash and beech trees bring us to a stream and the Fairy Bridge. Here it is the custom to salute the fairies and say: 'Good morning Little People, how are you?' and you will have good luck for the rest of the day. This may be a bit embarrassing and Barrie-esque for Englishmen, but the Manx have a strong sense of the supernatural. It goes back to the Stone Age, Bronze Age, Iron Age of the Celts, and on to the Vikings and to mediaeval times. Monuments of all these periods scatter the island. Fairy Bridge marked the boundary of the rich Cistercian lands of Rushen Abbey, where once there may have been a Calvary at which travellers stopped to say a prayer, and this salute may be its survival. Certainly anyone living long enough on this haunted island will have a sense of former peoples still present, and of their beliefs in the pagan god who controlled the mists and brought them down when the Kingdom of Man was threatened with invasion. It is known that whenever an English monarch visits the island a mist comes down, as it last did on the arrival of George VI.

The island is full of handsome Georgian country houses standing behind limestone walls in wooded demesnes. I think of one I know on the way from the airport to Douglas.

It stands, a stucco classic building at the head of a wooded glen. Its garden windows look over ilex, tall rhododendrons, palms and beech trees, to a glimpse between steep hills of sea. Its high, elegant rooms have original William Morris papers. I think of another, The Nunnery, the biggest country house in the island, in a splendidly landscaped park which might have been laid out by Repton or Capability Brown, which comes down to the centre of Douglas. The house is in the Gothic style fashionable throughout the island at the beginning of the last century.

The hotel where I am staying in Douglas was once one of these houses. It was built by Buck Whaley, an Irish gambler who came, as many did in Georgian days, to the island to evade his creditors. In the morning, the low hoot of one of the Isle of Man steamers setting out from the harbour below for England awoke me to the cry of seagulls and the long, long view of Douglas Bay, the Naples of the North; two miles of front with horse-trams down the promenade; tall, bay-windowed boarding houses packed with North Country visitors; above them in the trees castle-like houses now become hotels, and brown and blue in the morning sun the chain of hills and mountains which divide this east coast from the west. The steam railway station at Douglas is a fanciful building of the eighties in shiny red brick, and the gold domes of its gateway terminate the vista of Atholl Street, the grand, professional Georgian street of the town. The gateway symbolises the adventure of exploring the island by steam train. The narrow gauge lines wind inland beside the streams, over little bridges and through cuttings and banks of fern and glimpses of waterfall. The rolling stock is old-fashioned. The speed is leisurely, for what need is there for hurry once we are safe in the island, and from the train you see more country, as you do in England, than from the road. At St John's junction for the line along the west coast to the north is Tynwald Hill. Here, on 5 July, Midsummer Day by the old calendar, the laws – passed by the Court of Tynwald, consisting of the Lieutenant Governor, the Bishop, Attorney General, the two Deemsters (or Judges), the Water Bailiff, Archdeacon and others and by the 24 Keys of the House of Keys in the previous year – are read out in English and Manx and thereafter become law. The procession to Tynwald Hill comes out of St John's Church down the straight avenue between the flags of England and Man. The Norse sword of state is carried with it, and the Governor takes his seat on the top of the mound and, in descending order of importance, the legislative body sits on the descending piers below him. From all over the island, from towns and remote crofts and rich farms and fishing ports, the Manx come in for this great holiday and, though there may be rain and mist on other parts of the island, the sun always shines on 5 July on Tynwald Hill. The place is hidden from the sea, though it is only two miles from Peel, and a smell of wood smoke and kippers greets the nose before we come to the winding, narrow streets of this sheltered fishing town, guarded by an island on which stand the castle and ruined cathedral of St German's. Peel must be the only city in the British Isles to have its local paper, the *Peel City Guardian*, hand-set. Between Peel and Bradda Head, which shelters the Victorian boarding houses of Port Erin, is the wild west coast of Man. Here, gorse and heather slope steeply to the rocky cliff edge. Here are wildness and quiet and a few crofts. You would not think Douglas, with its dance halls and theatres and casino and coloured lights, could be on the same island. In the evening you may see the drifters leaving Peel against the sunset for the herring fishing, and then back by train through the darkening glens till you come to the streams of coloured lights in Douglas Bay and the floodlit Tower of Refuge on its rocky island commemorating Sir William Hillary, founder of the Royal National Lifeboat Institution.

Another day we take the electric tram from Derby Castle out through fields and the Cornish-looking mining town of Laxey, with its giant waterwheel, to Ramsey and the north. You can change at Laxey at an Edwardian cast-iron station and take another tram to the top of Snaefell Mountain, and have tea on the summit, where the kettles boil extra fast because of the height. Ramsey regards itself as a more exclusive place than Douglas. It has a beautiful Georgian court house by George Steuart, the architect of the eighteenth-century Castle Mona in Douglas, once the residence of the Dukes of Atholl, before they sold the island to the British Government in 1829. Ramsey is a sheltered town with stucco terraces, and ilexes and palm trees and fuchsias, a wide harbour and a bleak promenade with a long pier. But it is north of Ramsey, towards the Point of Ayre and the little lanes of the parishes of Bride, Andreas, Jurby and Ballaugh that, for me, the best of the island is to be found. In most countries in the northern hemisphere, the northern pan is bleak and the southern warm and lush. In Man, it is the other way round. The range of mountains below Snaefell, cleft in two by Sulby Glen, the wildest, biggest and most Scottish part of the island, protects these flattish farming lands from the prevailing south-west wind. Trees grow high, farms are large, lanes wind past thatched cottages, whose stone walls are still kept dazzling white with limewash and whose gardens are bright with dahlias, roses and begonias. The beaches are wide and gold and empty and the sky a deepening blue. Strangest and most luxuriant of all are the Curraghs on the far side of the modern zoo. Here are overgrown grass lanes in primitive swamps, with bog myrtle either side of you, rare willows, large butterflies, and king ferns whose enormous fronds have the primitive look of what grew in coal forests, and in the hot stillness one is back on the earth before man came to it.

The old capital of the island is Castletown, near the airport. Architecturally, it is the finest town in the island and still has the quality of a capital about it. If you are going 'up to the town' in the Isle of Man, it does not mean you are going to Douglas, but to Castletown. You 'go down' to Douglas. The castle which gives its name to the town is Rushen, the most complete thirteenth- and fourteenth-century castle in the British Isles with keep, outer gatehouse and curtain wall. The streets are full of Georgian houses. The Nautical Museum tells you of the great days when the Custom law in the Isle of Man had the advantage over that in Britain. The quaysides have wharves and secret stairs. The church, with box pews and galleries, looks out on to the square and the Greek column erected to Governor Smelt. The old House of Keys, now a bank, is not far off, and the police station by Baillie Scott, one of the pioneers of modern architecture, though he would have hated to have been called such, is a model of harmonious building on a critical site. To the south-west comer of the island, the country flattens and the road seems more used on its way to Port St Mary, and then suddenly we climb up past Glen Chass, with its bracken, to the surviving Celtic farming settlement of Cregneash. Here are whitewashed cottages with gold straw thatch, sheep with four horns and a folk museum, the first open-air museum in the British Isles.

It shows you how the Manx lived before tourism became their main industry. Beyond Cregneash is Spanish Head, where cliffs fall sheer 200 feet into the sea, and acres of cliff top are gold and purple with gorse and heather and green streams of moss and bracken between boulders. There, across the dangerous sound is the Calf of Man, islanded and alone among seals and puffins and enormous seas.

The motto round the three legs of the Isle of Man means 'Whichever way you throw it, it will stand'. Through the centuries this lovely island has certainly been thrown about, from Celts to Vikings, from Vikings to Scots, from Scots to English kings, from English kings to the Stanley family and their descendants, the Dukes of Atholl, and from them to that glum thing, the English Treasury and its handmaiden, the Home Office. Yet still the island has maintained its independence and, far more than England, its natural beauty. People who have not been there think the Isle of Man is a windy, bleak place, with a dirt track round it for the TT racing, and a casino in a lesser Blackpool. How wrong they are.

The best of the

competent

Book Reviews

ഇൻ

Betjeman joined the *Telegraph*'s team of critics at the opening of 1951 as a reviewer of 'new fiction' and for most of the next decade he would regularly appear on the book review day of Friday with his thoughts on the novels he was presented with. Initially he reviewed every week, and he got through an awful lot of books in the process – 1951 would see him assess 168 works in the newspaper. After a couple of years, perhaps mercifully for him, the workload was shared and he would appear on a fortnightly basis, save for any holidays, until the end of 1958. The vast majority of the books he reviewed have been mostly forgotten – does anybody remember, say, *Happy is the House* by Winifred Mantle these days? The now little-read Ivy Compton-Burnett was also a favourite of his, and she popped up on a number of occasions. Indeed, it is interesting to note the number of works that received a Betjeman 'thumbs up' which have since vanished into the mists of time.

Perhaps even more noteworthy are certain 'modern classics' that rated little mention by Betjeman upon first publication – *The Catcher in the Rye*, for example, received barely over a hundred words, and Ms Mantle's work, cited above, received greater coverage and a more positive review than the rather more celebrated *The Day of the Triffids*. On most occasions Betjeman could find something positive to say about the books he received, and it was very rare for him to cast a notably damning judgement on a writer; even those who weren't to his taste he would often recognise as having an appeal to a different constituency of readers.

As the fifties progressed Betjeman would also be given non-fiction to review, mainly in the fields of railways and architecture, but also, and possibly rather surprisingly, poetry books. One wonders what other poets made of one of their fellows having such a public platform to judge their work...

Come the sixties and Betjeman effectively vanished as a reviewer, although the *Sunday Telegraph* occasionally used him. Indeed, the very last byline for Betjeman in the *Telegraph* archive is to be found in the *Sunday Telegraph* of 1 April 1979, where he reviewed a biography of early London Underground supremo Frank Pick; it is a shame that he should find the last book he reviewed for the newspapers 'rather stodgy reading'.

We start here with his first review for the *Telegraph*. Included thereafter are some well-known authors and works, as well as some rather obscurer ones. Taken together they encapsulate the Betjeman 'voice' of his time at the paper.

Incalculable Critic

10 January 1951

London Day by Day

෨ ෬

M r John Betjeman, who on Friday joins the *Daily Telegraph* as novel reviewer, called his first published work *Ghastly Good Taste*. It set the note for an odd, varied and highly distinguished career.

On the subject of architecture he has strong, if sometimes impish, views. Victorian Gothic has found in him a solitary but spirited admirer. In praise of the despised Suburbia he has written tender and melodious verse. On American girls' schools he is a leading authority. At different times he has been editor of an architectural journal, a film critic, a press attaché and a writer of guidebooks.

His wit is unfailingly agile and pleasantly astringent, and his judgements are always his own. As a critic he has the enormous merit of being incalculable.

PETERBOROUGH

***

Mayor and Priest

The Little World of Don Camillo,
Giovanni Guareschi

12 January 1951

෨ ෬

M any people, who are neither, are inclined to ally modern Russians with the Devil, and Papists with God. *The Little World of Don Camillo* shows how this can be a dangerous oversimplification, at any rate so far as Italian country people are concerned.

Don Camillo is the priest of a north Italian village. Peppone is its Communist mayor. Both are large men, with a large and wary respect for one another. For instance, when Don Camillo finds that some damned soul has tied crackers to the clappers of his church bells, he does not say a word, though he seethes with fury inside and goes to bed with a temperature. Next morning he steals the tommy gun the mayor had himself stolen during the war. And the matter is soon settled. The mayor, of course, had tied the crackers to the bells.

There are a series of such struggles between priest and mayor, and the odds are even in each fight. The mayor is not a Communist in the Bloomsbury sense of the word. He brings his baby to be baptised – which is not the practice of our English party members – but he insists on its being called 'Lenin Libero Antonio'. Don Camillo insists that it shall not be so called. The two large men settle the name with fisticuffs.

Don Camillo is no saint, he is tough, a poacher and hasty tempered. Peppone is a braggart and talks a lot of nonsense about liberty and community centres. But both love their neighbours, and by the end are devoted to each other; and we, as we read, grow devoted to them both.

I may have given an impression that this book is only light entertainment. It is more. The lively talks of Don Camillo with God at the altar of his prayers are humorous and real, not mawkish. On what he says in these prayers and on what answers he receives hangs the plot of each of these stories.

This is one of the few modern books which engenders a feeling of happiness and benevolence towards mankind, even of hope for humanity. The reason is that its author sees the human heart under the cassock or behind the public figure.

***

Edwardian Style

Randall and the River of Time, C.S. Forester

19 January 1951

໓໖

I was inquiring lately of someone who likes those novels by clever Europeans about dreams and symbols, whom he thought really good among living English novelists? He mentioned the usual unreadable ones and made the usual smart omissions, and then, to my surprise, added, 'C.S. Forester'. I say 'surprise' because I enjoy the Hornblower stories myself, and so do those of my acquaintance who cannot by a long chalk be called 'literary'. And then he added 'within his limits'.

Those limits are C.S. Forester's strength. He is a born storyteller. Forty years ago, in the high summer of the Edwardian novel, he would not have seemed so remarkable as he does now. He writes without pretension, and his sole object is to tell an exciting story in which characters and setting are faithfully drawn. He deals in action, not introspection. He believes that we are under Providence – that comes out in all his books. And what he writes seems, at the time of reading, to be quite true.

In *Randall and the River of Time*, now that I have put it down and thought it over calmly, I see much that is impossible. Randall is the son of a south London schoolmaster. The time is the 1914 war. As a subaltern of nineteen he invents an adaptation of a flare so widely used that his name becomes known throughout the Army. He marries a woman older than himself who is incapable of being faithful to him once he is demobilised. There is a manslaughter charge, an unsavoury case, and Randall becomes even better known than he was as an inventor.

It is improbable; but every character and event – Randall's self-sacrificing father, his shallow, hard little wife torn between lust and respectability, the scenes of trench warfare, the trial at the Old Bailey – all have the impact of personal experiences. Mr Forester makes even the invention of a machine to sort wrinkled from smooth peas for the canning industry into something thrilling. With his gift of holding attention goes a power of presenting decent English middle-class people as they really are. He does not mock their inarticulateness and respectability.

*****

Ghost Stories

The Haunter of the Dark and Other Tales of Terror,
H.P. Lovecraft

16 February 1951

℘ ℭ

G host stories are an English speciality. Those by M.R. James are the best ever written. They are beautiful and concise. Their characters are full-blooded, and the ghosts are skinny and evil and leave much to the terrified imagination. Next to James I would put E.F. Benson, H.R. Wakefield and Algernon Blackwood. Then there are the stories with a creepy atmosphere only, of which the greatest masterpiece is 'The Monkey's Paw', by W.W. Jacobs. And there are the long-drawn-out paralysing ghosts that Machen, Oliver Onions, Meade Falkner and Le Fanu have created.

But the Americans cannot do it, except for Henry James and Edith Wharton, and they became so Europeanised as to count as English writers. When I started *The Haunter of the Dark and Other Tales of Terror* by H.P. Lovecraft, I hoped that here might be someone of the James and Wharton school. But no. This is an unsubtle American book, with cobwebs, winding passages, terrible rites and vast pseudo-scientific and pseudo-archaeological imaginings.

The ten long stories in this book are all readable, but they are not frightening and not really so imaginative and poetical as those by M.R. James. They remind me too much of Boris Karloff and not enough of the devil.

Black Magic

The Cistern and the Fountain, Jean Matheson

Jean Matheson, on the other hand, is almost too anxious to introduce the devil into her entertaining first novel, *The Cistern and the Fountain*. Mrs Maudslie's husband ran away with all the jewels and the whole bank account. She was left with a large Scottish house, a young gardener and a grumbling maid. Ever so bravely she turned it into a guest house. For the first few chapters I was thinking we were in for a Scottish Angela Thirkell.

Then Jean Matheson gradually changes her tone. A wicked woman arrives who discovers the dark secrets of all these nice people. She practises black magic. She has an awkward session with the Episcopal priest, who drives the devil out of her, and all ends happily.

Here is a talented writer but she has produced an unremarkable novel. She might write ghost stories and she certainly can write good, light comedy. They do not, however, go together in the same novel.

***

Mr Coward's World

Star Quality, Noël Coward

4 May 1951

෨෬

There are six short stories, two of them almost of novel length, in *Star Quality*. Let me admit at once that Mr Coward does not write with uniform excellence. When he is recording conversation, you can hear the people speak. But in prose passages he is jerky and sometimes puts in too much needless detail. There are, for instance, so many gins and whiskies in these stories that the reader finishes feeling drunk.

That is a criticism I must make of this modest and excellent book. And it is a modest book. He has confined himself to the world he knows, except for one Blue Lagoon-style story. His characters are all from theatre, films and *Tatler*-ish people, mingled with a few cockneys whom he prefers, in his heart, to the rest.

The best story of all is the longest, and it gives its title to the book. It is about Lorraine Barrie, a famous actress, who lives in a mews house with pink walls and blue shutters off Knightsbridge.

I doubt if a description of a ruthlessly egocentric actress could be better done. We watch how she makes the author rewrite the last act, so that she is on the stage longer. We watch her fight and lose a battle to have an indifferent actress as her foil. We listen to the exaggerated stagey talk, we smell the greasepaint and shake with the hysteria.

Another story is about an English film star who remains in America for the war and takes part in war films. War work in Hollywood is described with calm irony.

'Lulu Frazer had volunteered to make a tour of personal appearances for the Red Cross and had designed for herself two uniforms, one for day work and one for night work and both in sharkskin.'

There is a tale about a pathetic couple, the British Resident and his wife, on a forgotten island: another about a woman who is terrified of flying by air and how tactless her friends are before the journey. Better than these is a short account of the wife of a professional funny man who does not find her husband's stories funny. The remaining story is a devastating picture of disillusion – a man who thinks he is still attractive to a woman who has, since he first knew her, become a famous actress.

Of course there is something dated and touching about the elderly rebels of these stories. They are so anxious to flout the conventions. And there are so few conventions left to flout. But such period charm adds to their authenticity.

***

Priestley Comedy

Festival at Farbridge, J.B. Priestley

11 May 1951

Let me think of all I can say in favour of this new novel of Mr Priestley's, *Festival at Farbridge*. There is well-sustained suspense. This is the plot. The three chief characters are out of work but all good sorts. Laura, the dark-haired typist, has just been sacked from the estate agent's office at Farbridge. Theodore has come from Malaya to see England. He is a blond, prize-fighting type, who has also read Shakespeare and had a Chinese grandmother. The Commodore is an elderly pipe-smoking adventurer, temporarily out of a job.

The three of them combine to make the Farbridge Borough Council reverse its decision not to have a festival this year. They succeed, despite great opposition, and are appointed organisers. The festival is a success, but only just. By the end of it Theodore is going to marry Laura. The Commodore, though already married, is, with Mr Priestley's blessing, going to live with a married woman.

With nearly 600 pages and 125 subsidiary characters, this book is a conscientious attempt to return to the old comic novels in the tradition of Dickens and Thackeray, though not to their morality. All characters are called in and accounted for, married off or disgraced, according to whether they are friends or enemies.

Some of them are amusing and truthful portraits. The local education officer who always says 'Erce' is absolutely first class. Then there is the estate agent who poses as a squire; Capt. Mobbs, the hard-drinking, courageous, but not very cultivated Conservative agent; the Field Marshal, who collects ceramics; the balmy peer and his drunken daughter; Mrs Coote with her public welfare work and her untidy house full of uninhibited offspring; the humourless economists. And here and there are illuminatingly amusing remarks.

Bad Temper

But I dislike much of the book, because so much of it is bad-tempered. The slapstick comedy too often deviates into theatrical 'business'. None of the chief characters is alive. Mr Priestley shares, at any rate, this with Dickens – he cannot draw good women. Nor can he draw good men. The only people he can describe accurately and sometimes brilliantly, at other times clumsily, are those he dislikes or despises, and they are many.

His chief indication that he approves of a man is that he smokes a pipe. There are at least five pipe-smokers in the novel, all approved of by the author. A pipe and a stiff whisky and a leather armchair, socialism combined with plenty of brass, and taciturn silence broken by rudeness, seem to be the qualifications for a hero. Qualifications for villainy are interest in the Third

Programme and documentary films, a critical faculty, liking modern literature or art or verse-drama, or being Conservative or Communist.

In fact, Mr Priestley takes such a self-pitying pride in being the plain man (which he is not) throughout this book, that he would have us all a nation of robots — whisky-sodden males or flighty 'frippets', living only for the day, and with no ideals but brass-getting and physical relaxation.

The great comic novelists wrote out of love for their fellow creatures and hatred of oppression. Mr Priestley's book sounds peevish and disappointed beside them. It is long, which the libraries like, and topical. It the work of a real craftsman, but it is not healthy.

***

Mr Nevil Shute

Round the Bend, Nevil Shute

15 June 1951

&)Cß

Nevil Shute is at the moment about the most successful English novelist. He appears in a Uniform Edition at 6s. a time, even before he is middle-aged. He writes a book a year. In the sun-smitten bookshops near the equator the English books displayed are generally Churchill's *History of the War*, the novels of A.J. Cronin, and *A Town Like Alice* by Nevil Shute, and soon they will be displaying *Round the Bend* by Nevil Shute.

Let me try to find out why he is so popular. *Round the Bend* is written in the most awful got-begotten style. When I got going reading it, I got the impression I'd better get down to getting myself disinfected of all these gots before I got reviewing the book. The prose sounds rather as though it had been spilled into a Dictaphone. But then it is many years since a use of beautiful English earned a man fame.

He has been called a prince of storytellers. But he is not a Kipling. In *Round the Bend* he strains his story-telling talent to capacity. All that happens is that the one man, the narrator, rises to commercial eminence, and another man, the hero, dies. The love interest is unimportant. Yet he holds attention to the last page.

Shute's success cannot be due only to his power of telling a story. Others have that gift. It is also choice of subject; he appeals to manliness in people. The setting of *Round the Bend* is commercial airways. Tom Cutter started life in Sir Alan Cobham's air circus, became an RAF pilot, and married unhappily. His wife died, and after the war he started with one air taxi in Arabia. He gradually built up a fleet of aeroplanes by bravery, integrity and hard work. A young, self-made Englishman running air taxis in the East is perhaps the nearest approach we can make in these days of semi-peace to the Elizabethan sea captains.

A Holy Man

On Cutter's staff is a pilot and ground engineer, born in Penang with a Chinese father and Russian mother. He is a British subject, more Asiatic than European. This man, called Connie, presents us with the colour problem. We realise he is a more serious and trustworthy man than most pure whites. Colour bars are consciously broken down throughout the book.

The main theme is religion. Twenty years ago novels had to be about politics to be thought profound. Now they are about religion. Connie is regarded as a very holy man by Moslems and Hindus alike. He teaches religion to Asiatic staff at commercial aerodromes all over the East. He is thought by some to be divine. His teaching is but vaguely hinted at; it is something to do with work being prayer, and the proper care of aeroplane engines being all for the Glory of God. It is a bit indefinite; but so is 'popular religion'.

Nevil Shute extols the virtues we Westerners admire, of constancy and courage. He does not sound priggish or false, because he is obviously sincere. He is not a self-styled 'plain' man with loud, dull opinions. He is humbler than that. He writes because he wants to give us hope. He does not write literature, but I think he succeeds in his mission.

***

Brittany Holiday

A Dark Stranger, Julien Gracq

22 July 1951

෨෬

A Dark Stranger, by Julien Gracq, is about a summer holiday on the coast of Brittany. A party of young people is dominated by a half-English Anglomaniac. The publishers tell us that the writer recalls Edgar Allan Poe and Proust; that he evokes an obsessive, dramatically charged atmosphere. Here is a specimen of the atmosphere so charged:

> 'Irene — not here, no, please, not here.'
> 'Come.' She drew him against her on the settee, gently pressing her breasts against his chest. Under her black mask, with a fierce immobility, a feeble spot of liquid light on her dark lips, she leaned her face over him with a sleep-walker's slowness. Jacques felt a surge of brute desire leap within him.
> 'Kiss me.' He melted, wrapped in a moist over-whelming warmth.

The book has so many obvious misprints that no proof reader ought to have passed it. It is a disgrace to the once high standard of British book printing.

***

More Nancy Mitford

The Blessing, Nancy Mitford

27 July 1951

౸య

All who have read *The Blessing*, by Nancy Mitford, will have laughed a good deal. Unreadability is often mistaken for profundity, and what is translated is assumed to be better than what is written in English, so Nancy Mitford is passed over lightly.

She is deliberately frivolous. She laughs about 'serious things' like Anglo-American relations and the atom bomb in her new novel. She is contemporary and immensely readable. She is unforgivably entertaining. She does not instruct. I am quite certain there is no hidden allegory or moral teaching behind her writing. So when I say that *The Blessing* is not in my opinion as good as *The Pursuit of Love*, that is not saying it is not good by comparison with most modern novels. It is.

But the plot is frustrating. Grace is a rich smart English girl who has married a rich smart Free Frenchman during the war. They are very fond of each other. After the war she settles in France with her husband and their one son, Sigismond, known as 'the blessing'. Grace and her husband separate owing to his physical infidelities. The story is of 'the blessing's' determined attempts to keep his parents apart because he has so much better a time with each parent separately. Such a plot is a little too heart-rending to be in keeping with the funny characters who take parts in it. Fortunately, neither Grace nor her husband, nor the precious child, are exactly human.

Human Silliness

The humour of the book is in the minor characters, of whom there are plenty. An American with the superb name of Hector Dexter is a powerful bore. Here he is at the dinner table: 'Our visit to London was an integral success. I went to learn about the present or peace-time conditions there and to sense the present or peace-time mood of you Britishers, and I think I fully achieved both these aims.' Nancy Mitford lends herself to quotation. Here is a snobbish French collaborator talking at dinner:

> 'In wars,' said Grace, 'you rather expect battles.'
>
> 'Not in one's own chateau, my dear! How we were relieved when the Germans went away — just packed up one day and went — and we saw two nice young Guards officers of good family, Etonians, coming up the drive.'

It is this gift for revealing, briefly and vividly, stretching acres of human silliness that makes Nancy Mitford so worth reading. She is an affectionate, unbitter humorist who delights to shock the pretentious.

***

Deckchair Reading

My Cousin Rachel, Daphne du Maurier

3 August 1951

ᔕᒧᑕᘔ

The new Daphne du Maurier, *My Cousin Rachel*, has all the ingredients of a bestseller. The story is good and carries the reader through the padding. The padding itself is flattering to the intelligence, for it is vaguely psychological. Also there is some horror and storm introduced to give an atmosphere of mystery and profundity. Then the setting is vaguely historical and Cornish. But the language is not so historical.

'I am no child,' says the narrator, the hero of the book who is in love with his cousin Rachel. 'I am five-and-twenty years,' he continues in the antient style, but concludes 'all but three blasted months', and we know then it is Daphne du Maurier and not Sir Walter Scott who is writing.

I do not want to be snobbish and superior about this book. It is a very good piece of deckchair reading. It catches the escapist mood of the moment, and is not too like life to be upsetting. I must add that the author has been unusual in making Rachel, her heroine, not wholly good but a mixture, as real people are, of good and evil. The rest of the characters are stock.

***

A Play-Novelette

Burning Bright, John Steinbeck

10 August 1951

ಹಾ ೮೩

John Steinbeck's latest works, *Of Mice and Men* and *The Moon Is Down*, have been short. So is his new book, *Burning Bright*. In a foreword he explains that in this and in those two previous books he is attempting a new form of literature. He is trying to write a play as a novel. Plays he finds difficult to read. Most of us will agree. So are most long modern novels, but I am not sure that the 'play-novelette', though shorter, is much easier.

Its chief difference from a novel is that each of Mr Steinbeck's chapters is called an act, and there are three acts to his book. The scene of each act changes. Exits and entrances are carefully arranged; dialogue is as though spoken to an audience and not to a reader.

The first act introduces the characters. Scene a circus tent. Old acrobat with young wife. Young wife loved by acrobat's young partner, a smug athlete with no sensibilities. Love not returned, but old acrobat badly wants a child by his young wife and cannot produce one. Young wife knows this and loves her old husband so much she decides to have a child with the smug young acrobat as father.

By the end of the play the old husband has discovered what she has done. He forgives her. The moral of the play – and it is very much a morality play – is that human beings are more important than impeccable ancestry.

Mr Steinbeck draws his moral conclusion forcefully for all to understand. But I do not think his book is 'powerful' as was his *The Grapes of Wrath*. The talk is too literary. And so is the form. It smacks of the study and the typewriter, for all its sincerity, and not of life. But the form he employs might be copied with advantage by those Americans who write long sagas about North v. South or old families coming over with the *Mayflower*. It is at least concise and as unwasteful of paper.

The Poor of Merseyside

No Language but a Cry, H.J. Cross

H.J. Cross is a schoolmaster who was for years teaching at a rough school on Merseyside. Clearly he wrote his novel *No Language but a Cry* with a burning love for his pupils and with a sense of outrage at those who sit in Parliament and other clubs generalising about child delinquency.

By great good fortune he unites with his love for his subject the ability to tell a story and to sketch a scene and mood in a few words. His book is not sham proletarian but full of authentic observation – the smell of seaweed, coal dust and engine oil, the blasphemy, the black markets, the steamy cafés, the picture on the kitchen wall sliding crooked as the trains go by outside, the staircase toughs, the bullying on bombed sites and arid recreation grounds.

Against this setting, Mr Cross tells the moving story of Mickey, a Merseyside boy, the child of a broken home. I do not recollect a better description of tenement life among those thundering cobbled streets, pubs and pawnbrokers and smoke.

Dead End Kids

Mickey's father was a huge tough whom the Army had ruined by making him discontented with simplicity. He starts to steal cloth from the docks, leaves his slatternly but loving wife, and Mickey who also loves him. Mickey finds consolation in the companionship of a gang of older boys who involve him in a crime far worse than his father's pilferings. The other side of Mickey is discovered by the art master at his school. He can draw and he loves drawing.

Unfortunately it is not so easy for the reader to believe in Mickey's artistic genius. But it is not necessary. Mr Cross has accomplished his purpose. He has shown that many of those luckless sham 'Dead End Kids' whom we dismiss as 'young hooligans' may be like Mickey, the children of selfish and stupid separated parents or else illegitimate.

He has shown that it is not the schools which are to blame for children going wrong. Day schools of big towns do not keep the children for enough of the day to alter their characters. It is the parents, uncertain of temper, tired, disillusioned, and taken to theft or drink or adultery, who are to blame.

If we knew this before, at least we can remember it now from the story of Mickey. Yet this is not an angry or self-righteous book. It brings out the love and help the poor and oppressed give to one another in emergency. It is thrilling and tender, worth a shelf of bestsellers.

The Rich of America

The Catcher in the Rye, J.D. Salinger

There could hardly be a greater contrast with Mickey than the 'I' who narrates *The Catcher in the Rye*, by J.D. Salinger. He is an American boy of sixteen, child of rich parents, and just sent away from his fourth school for refusing to work. He tells us of the few days after he leaves his school and before he goes home to fall ill.

The manner of telling is conversational and full of American slang. But the boy himself, through all his strangeness and his chronic indolence, is somehow sane and charming. The book carries its reader along through the force of the narrator's personality and outlook.

***

Tough Sea Story

The Cruel Sea, Nicholas Monsarrat

31 August 1951

ଚ୦ ଓଃ

The Cruel Sea has the hallmarks of bestsellerdom. Book Society Choice, Book of the Month in America, all editions sold out before the book is written, highly commended by public libraries, such boosting is no recommendation to an envious cynic like your reviewer.

Indeed, he knows that semi-official committees of taste can, at their best, discourage the circulation of absolute tripe. But they are unlikely to recommend a work of genius. They have to think of Mrs Everybody, who mistrusts genius but now apparently has little objection to dirt. There is a surprising lack of reticence about sex in *The Cruel Sea*. Indeed, the author seems deliberately to set out to shock his readers with the shore life of some sailors and with gruesome details of killing, as this about a depth-charge exploded among drowning men:

> Men floated high on the surface like dead goldfish in a film of blood. Most of them were disintegrated, or pulped out of human shape. But half a dozen of them, who must have been on the edge of the explosion, had come to a tidier end: split open from chin to crutch, they had been as neatly gutted as any herring. Some seagulls were already busy on the scene, screaming with excitement and delight. Nothing else stirred.

Strong and tough stuff, no doubt. Something to bring things home to Mrs Everybody, who is supposed not to know about the horrors of war. This author's contempt for all except physical action, his admiration of human ferocity, and his dislike of those who speak and write make one wonder why he was so inconsistent as to write a book himself. But the wonder is soon dispelled by appreciation.

He wrote this book out of a deep affection for his fellow officers in corvettes and frigates. It is this affection which carries one through the 400 pages of grey and closely printed text. He is at his best when describing convoys and action against U-boats. His two chief characters, Ericson, the commander and hero, Lockhart, his No. I and the hero-worshipper, are too good to be true. But his subsidiary characters, the officers who are more briefly sketched and whose backgrounds, whether Birmingham or Birkenhead, are so swiftly and touchingly portrayed — these come to life.

The action takes place between 1939 and the end of the war — first in a corvette which is sunk, then in a frigate. It is an excellent piece of naval journalism, much of it obviously based on bravely met experience. But it lacks the reticence and modesty of the older generation, and I turn with relief to the less angry and equally vivid writing of Bartimeus.

In the Future

The Day of the Triffids, John Wyndham

I f the future of this earth is to be as dreary as most people say then books about it are unlikely to be heartening. Mr John Wyndham, in *The Day of the Triffids*, imagines a world with the human race almost wiped out by atomic warfare. Mortals are blind. 'Triffids' are purposive stringing plants which uproot themselves from the earth and feed on decaying human flesh. As human beings are blind they cannot escape these stalking monsters whose object is to kill them. The story ends with a faint ray of hope. It is an imaginative tale spoiled by too much moralising from a man and a woman whom the author cannot make real.

***

Film Star's Novel

Round the Rugged Rocks, David Niven

14 December 1951

ᚨ ᚲ

D avid Niven obviously wrote *Round the Rugged Rocks* because he enjoyed doing it and not because he wanted to prove his versatility or literary skill. And he communicates his enjoyment; at least he did to me. The story is of an ex-Army officer who is 'willing to go anywhere, do anything'. He falls in love several times; he goes to America in charge of a valuable bulldog intended to advertise a dog food uneatable even by dogs; he tries a number of odd jobs there, and marries a very charming girl who is becoming a film star.

He then becomes an even more glamorous film star himself, nearly losing his wife in the process. Mr Niven has an affection for real people, he sees the funny side of things, and he sees through shams like publicity. His book is rather too much on the same cheerful note to sustain the story, but it is livelier and therefore better than the journalistic novels which appear at the rate of about twenty-five a week to be swallowed by the twopenny libraries.

***

Compton Mackenzie

The Rival Monster, Compton Mackenzie

18 January 1952

೫ುಀ

The Rival Monster is about Compton Mackenzie's sixty-ninth book. He himself is sixty-nine and he is still well up to form. The Loch Ness monster is thought to have been killed by a flying saucer. Its mate has gone bellowing in search of consolation to the Outer Isles of Great and Little Todday. Ben Nevis, the Highland Chieftain, is angered at the beast's desertion of the mainland and plans an expedition to Todday to haul it back. Paul Waggett, the pompous, unpopular and property proud London businessman who owns Todday, is angered too. He does not believe in the monster and he fears the rumour of its presence will encourage tourists.

It does. The novel, besides a full chorus of 'Garlic'-speaking natives, has cockney visitors, young lovers, hikers, scientists, journalists and BBC men, all on the stage at the final discovery of the beast in a cave on an uninhabited island. It is all good Highland horseplay, hearty fun rather than barbed wit. The pleasure it gives consists not in aphorisms but in fantastic situations.

The excellence of Compton Mackenzie as an entertainer is so often overlooked that had I space I would have liked to remind you of some former books by this much read but little praised man, from that marvellous evocation of late Victorian and Edwardian England in *Sinister Street* and the witty and affectionate picture of the Church of England given in *The Altar Steps*, to the fun of this recent Highland series.

His energy is the unflagging effort of a good story-teller and a good constructor with an ear for dialogue and prose. Most of his earlier books are out of print and unobtainable, either pulped or closely guarded. I think this is because he is, under the surface, a modest man whose writing seems ephemeral. He is like the black and white illustrator as opposed to the oil painter. His work will be more appreciated and valued the further it is away from us.

He is so faithful an illustrator of his times that to reread his earlier a work is like looking through back volumes of *Punch* or *The Illustrated London News*. It has the true period flavour. It is so much of its time that, like Trollope and Sherlock Holmes, it will continue to be appreciated when more pretentious writers are forgotten.

***

In London, SW1

Excellent Women, Barbara Pym

14 March 1952

&℃

B arbara Pym is a splendid humorous writer. She knows her limits and stays within them. She writes about the world which is much bigger than people suppose, of professional men — clergymen, doctors' widows, the higher but not the top grades of the Civil Service, naval officers and their wives, gentlewomen who are not yet quite distressed.

There are those who may find *Excellent Women* tame, with its fussing over church bazaars, 'high' and 'low' churchmanship, a boiled egg for lunch and a cup of tea before going to bed, but to me it is a perfect book. The setting is London, SW1, neither the smart nor the slummy part of it. The narrator, Mildred, is a vicar's daughter of about thirty, not bad looking but very dim, and still unmarried.

We leave the book happily wondering whether Mildred will marry her high church vicar or an inarticulate anthropologist who had asked her to meet his mother. Miss Pym's chief characters and her lesser ones are all carefully observed and wittily described. She is not sarcastic but always dry and caustic. Conscious charm by a professional ladies' man, quarrelsomeness from an old school friend, rows about where to put the lilies about the chancel at Easter, are subjects which suit her acid powers of description. *Excellent Women* is England and, thank goodness, it is full of them.

***

A Modern Morality

Root of Evil, Doreen Wallace

21 March 1952

൧Ⳣ

*R*oot of Evil is a modern morality. Doreen Wallace always writes moralities. Her books are quite on their own and I like them very much. Former novels have been about poor country people trying to rise above their circumstances and generally failing to do so.

In *Root of Evil* she returns to this theme. John Rowey is a thatcher who marries Jane, the daughter of a small farmer. They adopt an illegitimate half-brother of John called Joe. As oi hev no knowledge of Suffolk doyalect, bor, oi can't say whether their talk be roight. But they do tall incomprehensibly broad sometoimes. When John and Jane have a son of their own they determine to make him into a gentleman.

Young Bernard is good-looking and clever. His schoolmistresses dote on him as much as his parents and young half-uncle do. He wins scholarships from the local grammar school to Oxford. There he mixes with a set of ballet and poetry appreciators, and without being exactly ashamed of his origin he manages to conceal it. But his end is tragic.

Doreen Wallace is a sort of down to earth Dean Farrar, less obvious than he but as certain of Christian ethics. Judging hastily, one might think she intended her novel to condemn modern education as the root of evil. But this is not so. She condemns education which is just learning facts and 'trends' and a means to a dull office job, and not what it ought to be, the means of telling a growing person how to find himself and to live fully.

Bernard Rowley never had a chance. His father wanted to make him a 'gentleman'. His mother was kind but weak. His half-uncle was equally kind. All three were proud because he spoke nicely and was good at book learning, and that seemed to them worth paying for. His teachers were out for the honour of their school, or in love with him, or saw education in terms of the cash it would bring in later. And Bernard himself became that most defenceless thing, an intellectual with no roots.

Doreen Wallace knows what she means. She is moral without being mawkish. If her chief characters are a bit larger than life, all brain, all unselfishness or all pride, no matter. She makes her points convincingly in this disturbing story.

***

From the French

The Little Misery, Francois Mauriac

4 April 1952

The title of the latest Mauriac, *The Little Misery*, is an understatement. Into just over one hundred widely printed handsome pages he has crammed enormous misery. But Mauriac's gloom is not unhealthy. It stimulates after it depresses.

This is because Mauriac writes from a point of view. He is a Christian with a strong sense of good and evil. Unfortunately he seems to find evil more interesting to write about than good. Villains of fiction are usually more credible than heroes, and Paula, the villainess of this novel, is credible enough.

She is a bourgeoise who, in order to ally herself with the aristocracy, marries a baron who is a good-natured idiot. She hates her little son who is backward like his father. The boy finds security only with the servants and his father and grandmother. A Left-wing schoolmaster starts to make the boy happy by giving him lessons, but withdraws almost immediately. Son and father drown themselves after this, and we are left with Paula dying of cancer, without belief in a future life or a judgement. She is not sorry that she has driven her husband and son to their deaths; she could not help it. She only repents of the stupidity of her marriage. Under the morphine which is so bad for her liver, she wishes she had taken a strong, healthy man to her bed.

The only good that seems to come from all this misery is that the Left-wing schoolmaster deeply regrets he did not go on teaching the son. He might have saved him. This softens his ambitious, materialist nature. For all his gloom, there is not complete despair in Mauriac. He purges himself and his readers with pity for his benighted creations.

Farm in Flanders

The House by the Canal, Georges Simenon

There are two short novels by Simenon in *The House by the Canal*. He is not a moralist. He is a story-teller with a gift for atmosphere and character. The first, longer and better story gives its name to the book. A neurotic young girl from Brussels comes to live in a damp farm on a canal in Flanders with her country cousins. The two brothers fall in love with her. Both are louts. She marries the one who is a cad, and the better lout kills her.

The second story is more cheerful. It is about a group of escaped Belgian fishermen billeted in La Rochelle early in the war. Through tragedy and difficulty they achieve happiness, and outwit French officialdom and Nazi occupation.

Why bother, you may ask, to review two such dismal writers as these, and not even English? Because they do not wallow in tragedy. Because they are not escapists holding up a never-never land to people who want a 'nice book'. Because they both write briefly in this age which imagines that in fiction length is strength. Because both are well served by their respective translators, Gerard Hopkins and Geoffrey Sainsbury.

***

Sansom and Kipling

A Touch of the Sun, William Sansom

25 April 1952

৪০ ০৪

William Sansom's short stories, *A Touch of the Sun*, remind me of Kipling. He has the versatility, the ear and the sense of construction of that great man. He lacks Kipling's decided point of view, Kipling's admiration of the virtue of moral courage and perseverance. He is no Empire builder.

This contemporary amorality may make Sansom's writing unattractive to an older generation. Also he is not always up to form. From the light flutter of 'Plain Tales from the Hills' to the wonderful and horrible 'Mary Postgate' or that imaginative masterpiece 'The Gardener' (whose whole point depends on one short unobtrusive sentence), all Kipling's short stories succeed. Most of William Sansom's do.

Therefore I find *A Touch of the Sun* is an event in my reviewing life. Week after week I notice what I think the best of the competent middlebrow output from which I select. Week after week I am inclined to lower my standards by thinking 'this one is better than last week's best, so it must be first class', until I come up against a book like this of Sansom, which is so much better than the average 'excellent' of my reviews that I begin to remember what 'good' means.

Range of Selling

To begin with, Sansom can throw himself and his reader with him deep into such various worlds: English visitors to Venice; sunstroke in Gibraltar; stranded in Paris; mountaineering in the Tyrol; a London suburban flower shop – to quote a few settings in this book. 'Impatience' has a tense razor fight between two rival cheap barbers in the West End of London. Equally effective in the same story is the description of a Thé Dansant on a Sunday in a Mayfair hotel, when the East End moves west for a stately revel. The old theme of a lonely small boy in an empty house unconsciously outwitting a burglar has surely not been more frighteningly done than in 'The Face at the Window'.

For the story of a practical joke with a deadly dénouement in the last sentence, I commend 'The Smile'. Notice the skill with which Sansom introduces a strange atmosphere to this story by making the narrator one of the public waiting in the Poste Restante department of the Paris Central Post Office: 'An air of tragedy hangs about the pigeon-holes, about people without addresses, about the meek queue that has gathered from all over Paris for the letters that will change their lives and that never come.'

Notice, too, the Dornford Yates quality of tea-party talk in the suburban love story called 'On Stony Ground'.

***

Talented Newcomer

Mr Nicholas, Thomas Hinde

2 May 1952

೫ ೞ

Thomas Hinde, who wrote *Mr Nicholas*, is twenty-five years old. I think at twenty-five people can still remember and describe the bruises of youth. Older writers flood their youth with a golden sunlight and forget the suffering or magnify the pain, forgetting the jokes. I do not see how its author can write a better novel. If his second is as good he will indeed be a brilliant star.

Mr Nicholas is one of those particularly awful types who are affectionately described as 'big boys at heart', which is another way of saying they are cases of arrested development. There he is, still athletic, keen on a game of tennis, calling his wife 'old lady' and his sons 'old man' – 'Shut the door old man, I want to have a serious little chat with you' – there he is picking dandelions out of the lawn. And when you are cleaning your teeth in the morning there he is in the bathroom saying for the hundredth time: 'How often have I told you, old man, to turn round and clean your teeth into the lavatory, not into the basin?'

Wherever you are in the house he pervades it. His amours, his hearty jokes, his sudden violence, his self-pity are I suppose common to most of us who are middle-aged. We forget, smelling of gin and tobacco, guzzling and laughing loudly, how embarrassing and distasteful we can be to our children. Mr Nicholas is a terrible warning.

He crushes his eldest son into nonentity, he martyrises his wife, he drives his second son into the clutches of an elderly and undesirable half-pay captain, he turns his youngest son into a premature cynic. And, of course, he regards himself as perfect.

Mr Hinde writes briefly and simply. He takes the point of view of Mr Nicholas's children (aged fifteen, seventeen and eighteen).

> Owen tipped his chair. He had skill at being maddening and didn't hesitate to use it. He wanted the dog [the family was discussing buying one] but at the moment he wanted more to be unreasonably forbidden it.

He understands these early adult uses and emotions. He wisely leaves us to deduce the inner thoughts of Mr Nicholas. So furious does one become with Mr Nicholas, and so clearly does he stand out in our imagination, that one wants to take up the book and fling it at him. Then one realises he is in his pages, so one can't. This would be a triumph for an experienced author, and is most unusual in a young one.

***

A Novelist with an Acute
Sense of Observation

Hemlock and After, Angus Wilson

18 July 1952

৪০৫৪

*H*emlock and After is an outstanding book. But it is outstandingly frank about matters which cause some people to bring out horsewhips, and others to dial 999. Still more may write to the editor suggesting my dismissal for recommending a book about a small, 'decadent and unhealthy' set of people who are not worthy of description.

The innocent and good may find *Hemlock and After* incomprehensible. Since most of us are neither, we are sure to find in it a power of observation which would make us terrified of meeting the author, Angus Wilson. He would, we feel, know all about us, how we had behaved in the nursery, how we treat our wives, and what our most shameful thoughts are.

These qualities of observation alone make Angus Wilson an outstanding writer. He is mercilessly accurate and never dull. And he has an ear for dialogue, and a nice sense of the novel as a neat story which needs suspense and a neat conclusion.

Bernard Sands is a successful elderly novelist. He is so liberal-minded and omniscient that he is overwhelming. His wife Ella has retreated into a nervous breakdown. He has alas been so disturbingly natural with his children that his journalist daughter is a bright little bore, and his son a politically minded prig with a dull, domineering wife. Bernard has just persuaded the government to open a country house as a home for young writers.

A Modern Socrates

Most of the book leads up to the opening-day ceremony which proves a disaster. Bernard dies soon afterwards, and the epilogue is a disillusioning picture of the blasting of his hopes. It is like life and it shows little faith in the goodness of human nature. Bernard himself, the modern Socrates, has the ancient Greek interest in young men. But he is a man of high principles.

Not so are all those he meets. Bernard himself never emerges so clearly as the lesser characters. His effeminate young friend Eric, with his thoroughly selfish mother who takes pains to make herself out a lovely lady, really broad-minded and deeply unselfish; the coarse and sinister Mrs Curry who is a true corrupter of youth in the criminal sense; the flashy spiv Ron Wrigley; Terence the hard little theatrical designer, all talent and no heart; Bernard's sister Isobel, a Professor of English Literature – 'though she never quite admitted it even to herself, she had ceased to respond to any work of literature soon after she began her academical career'; Louie, her outspoken and keen young Communist friend – these are some of about fifty closely observed people.

They never bore because they are all alive. They never muddle the reader, because Mr Wilson can manage his characters and keep his story going. There is one depressing thing about them: they are almost all unpleasant in one way or another. Those who are not unpleasant are merely vague. Its lack of hope is the book's one weakness, a weakness which not even the compassion of the author for his characters can strengthen.

***

John Steinbeck's Long Novel of Californian Settlers

East of Eden, John Steinbeck

28 November 1952

෨෮෨

S teinbeck, the author of *The Moon Is Down*, *The Grapes of Wrath* and *Of Mice and Men* has the gift of readability. To some he may seem vast and profound.

In *East of Eden* his grandeur verges, for me, on the grandiose. 'I believe there is one story in the world, and only one, that has frightened and inspired us,' says Mr Steinbeck on his 359th page: '... Humans are caught – in their lives, in their thoughts, in their hungers and ambitions, in their avarice and cruelty, and in their kindness and generosity, too – in a net of good and evil.'

Most people will agree about the net, which may more technically be called 'original sin'. But I should have thought that what frightened people was not the battle on earth, but the thought of eternity beyond it, and what inspired a good many millions for the last two thousand years has been the knowledge of God become Man at Bethlehem.

Good and Evil

I do not mean to say anything so silly as that all large novels have to have a Christian theme to achieve greatness. But their authors have to have a firm philosophy of life to give their work proportion. Mr Steinbeck's battle of good and evil is not enough, though it is certainly a more realistic basis for a novel than many theories of human perfectibility. But it has led him to make his chief characters too black and white.

The evil woman who burns her parents alive, shoots her husband, corrupts, blackmails and murders young and old, is such a monument of pitiless lust and cruelty as can never have existed. She has not even a sentimental moment. All the births, beatings, murders, fights and deaths may give pleasure to library subscribers sitting in front of warm fires eating crumpets. But they seem to me too violent, and magnified out of all proportion.

Apart from this criticism, one cannot but admire the brainwork in the able construction of this novel. It is the familiar American theme of settlers and their grandchildren, and it covers the time from Abraham Lincoln to 1920. The setting is mostly Californian. We see the two half-brothers, the elder receiving his father's love and not wanting it, the other wanting his father's love and not receiving it.

The jealousy leads to a Cain and Abel situation which is repeated in the children of the next generation. There is much that is interesting, convincing, horrifying, and kind, in the pages of this book. Mr Steinbeck is especially good at evoking, without too many words, the atmosphere of remote communities and rough justice.

***

A Well-Informed Novel About the House of Commons

Who Goes Home, Maurice Edelman

23 January 1953

80C3

Who Goes Home, by Maurice Edelman, is a warm-hearted, well-informed and readable novel about our Parliament. Mr Edelman loves the House of Commons as some people love their old schools. He loves the intricate Gothic of Barry's masterpiece, the Palace of Westminster; he loves the ceremony; he enjoys the company of the members, in the bar and lobbies and in debate. It is this background, lovingly and well described, which becomes, perhaps intentionally, more important than the principal characters, who are the usual foreground of a novel.

The plot carries one swiftly along. It is about a young promising Minister (party unspecified, but probably Conservative) who is accused of accepting bribes from an American business corporation.

Some of the machinery of this plot is unreal — the political house party run by a mischief-making peer, a by-election, the suicide of the hero's wife, numerous divorces, and much bright talk which reads rather like the later Anthony Hope novels; but as soon as the characters come into the House, they come to life.

Vote of Censure

I finished this book feeling some regret for having so often slanged Members of Parliament. It reawakens one's respect for their institution and our system of government. When we read, in the final exciting chapters, of the Prime Minister's vote of censure on his Minister, undertaken because it is his duty to move the vote, and when we read of the Opposition leader's defence of this Minister, his political enemy, we realise how justice and humanity can be united in parliamentary debate. As the Prime Minister says of his revolutionary opponent:

> He thinks he is guiding our future. He isn't. Our future is guiding him. Our future guides him while our past pushes him along. Individualists will never make revolutions in Britain. We've gone too far. The impetus of our history is too great for our main direction ever to be changed. We may civilise our behaviour and improve our manners. But our future is already determined by our past.

Politicians, although they take up three-quarters of the space in our newspapers — and in my opinion that is too much — are not popular with us. Mr Edelman's novel enables me at least to think more kindly of them. But I hope they are less aimless in their private lives than he makes them out to be.

The Time of the Assassins, Godfrey Blunden

Godfrey Blunden's way of writing English in *The Time of the Assassins* is almost that of a translation. It is hard and strange. But so is his subject, the tale of the occupation of Kharkov by the Nazis in 1941. The book is ambitious, vast as the Ukraine, brutal, frightening, and, I regret to say, monotonous. By the time we reach the inconclusive finish, the Russians have re-entered Kharkov, and the implication is that there will be as much denunciation and mass slaughter as there was under the Nazis. The icy pessimism of this horrible story does not mean that it is not worth reading. I think it is if only for the fact that we can thank God that we did not live in Kharkov in those days. If you were a Party Member, you would have been hung upside down from your house window. If you were a traitor to the Nazis you might be hung up by a butcher's hook through your throat. If you were ill or Jewish, or didn't look like a German, you would be shot and shovelled away into a ditch.

But the book fails because it is unrelievedly inhuman. No one, except a schoolmistress who is subsequently shot, has any decent motives. No one, indeed, has any character as we understand character. 375 pages of this may be good value from the library point of view, as it takes a long time to read. But it does not for me perform any of the functions of a novel, which should sustain the reader to the end, even if in so doing it purges him with pity.

The Crown Princess, Brigid Brophy

B rigid Brophy's book of short stories, *The Crown Princess*, shows that she has good ideas and an understanding mind, astonishing in someone still in her early twenties.

The title story is, I think the best, for here she is dealing with a young girl. She describes the thoughts of a royal figure on her twenty-first birthday, how she has no private life for curious people to find out about, how she is an empty slave of her subjects.

I would also recommend 'Mrs Mandford's Drawing Room', which is a saddening story about the English character and the old and the new orders. In her longest story, 'The Financial World', Miss Brophy makes the mistake of trying to record the talk and emotions of men, which no woman should do (nor should a man try to do this of women). Her writing would be even more acute if she did not elaborate points which she has already made clear.

***

Bertrand Russell as Writer of Short Stories

Satan in the Suburbs and Other Stories,
Bertrand Russell

27 February 1953

ᗧᗤ

T here is something dehydrated about the short stories of Bertrand Russell, great man though he is and remarkable to turn to writing fiction at the age of eighty. But 'Satan in the Suburbs', the longest of the stories and the one which gives the title to his book, is the least successful because it is too cerebral.

It is the story of a doctor who settles down in Mortlake, causes a variety of rather smug and opinionated people to go off the rails, scandalise society, and drown themselves in a trough of self-humiliation.

One might say that there is not meant to be any heart in the story. But, if it is merely a story of ideas (and like all the stories it bristles with entertaining theories and elaborately constructed plots and sub-plots), one must answer that, in fiction, ideas are rarely enough. Probability must come in if human beings are used in the plot, or if not probability then a rich romantic atmosphere. This Bertrand Russell does achieve in 'The Corsican Ideal of Miss X', an adventure story that has a quality of Rider Haggard about it.

The best of the other stories, which makes the book worth buying in order to read it again, is called 'The Guardians of Parnassus'. It is a splendid tale of hate among university dons, and has the power of an immortal parable. I found myself less in sympathy with a long story about newspaper magnates, advertisers and scientists who wanted to govern the world again because it was overweighted with ideas.

Bertrand Russell lacks that streak of comfortable vulgarity which makes the ingenious scientific stories of H.G. Wells acceptable and probable. But he writes in a cultivated prose of clarity and decorum which strikes a refreshingly old-fashioned note on the ear, and which is suited to his style of wit: 'I was young in those days, and had not that stern devotion to moral principles which enables men to inflict torture without compunction.'

Adventures in Tomorrow,
Edited by Kendell Foster Crossen

Beside the science fiction stories in *Adventures in Tomorrow*, Bertrand Russell appears kind-hearted and probable. These stories, by a variety of American authors, are divided into Atomic Age, AD 1960–2,100, Galactic Age, AD 2,100–3,000, Stellar Age,

AD 3,000–10,000, Delphic Age, AD 10,000–100,000. They are only successful when their authors have imagination and some philosophy of life.

All the stories here are better than the usual science fiction which we pick up in lurid paperbacks in cheap stationers'. Most of their authors are not, thank goodness, dazzled by dreams of everything getting bigger and better. Sometimes, as in a story by Ray Bradbury of the end of the world in 1980 in fire and radioactivity, the effect is poetical, convincing, harassing, and indeed beautifully written, if anything so horrible can have the word beautiful applied to it.

But most of the stories I found profoundly boring. Travelling in space ships one does not expect to find the passengers talking in the commonplace language of the 6.15 from Waterloo.

No, the truth about science fiction, which is an American cult, is that it is no more convincing than most modern romantic historical fiction. The less talented among us can sink ourselves into the past, and men of genius like Sir Walter Scott even recreate it. But when the less talented project themselves into the future – of which, I hope you will forgive my pointing out, we know nothing – the result is ludicrous when not dull.

This is, alas, not a funny book. It contains four interesting writers, Ray Bradbury (easily the first), A.E. van Vogt, Walter van Tilburg Clark and Henry Kuttner. The rest are just the thing for schoolboys.

***

Comfortable Country House
Life of Fifty Years Ago

The Present and the Past, Ivy Compton-Burnett

27 March 1953

෯෬

*T*he Present and the Past is the thirteenth novel of this remarkable writer, Ivy Compton-Burnett. Her manner of writing has always been the same. The settings and situations have been somewhat similar, too – generally a background, as in this novel, of unhurried, comfortable country house life at the beginning of this century. The story here, as usual, is told in a series of laconic dialogues.

In this novel we have a husband and wife with five children and a large domestic staff. There is a neighbouring family, to one of whose children the husband had been married. But we are now in the regime of the second wife. The routine of the house is suddenly disturbed by the return of this first wife who wishes to see her children.

The Servants

In the past I have found Miss Compton-Burnett's unemotional and very clever writing something to admire but not always to enjoy. Advancing years have increased my enjoyment.

Her characters are sketched briefly and originally: Eliza, the nursery maid ('she had an uneducated expression and an air of knowledge of life that seemed its natural accompaniment'): Miss Bennet, the nurse whom the children loved 'not as themselves, but as the person who served their love of themselves, and greater love has no child than this'; the governess ('her life was divided between her conscience and her inclination: It was her concern to strike the mean between them, and her merit that she did so').

It may seem to some a weakness that Miss Compton-Burnett's formula for conversation is the same for the servants' hall, the drawing room and the nursery. Thus the boys:

'Has Father ever been fond of anyone?'
'Of both his wives, if the present one is to be believed.'

And thus the servants:

'... I am a confidential servant.'
'For what that is worth,' said Halliday.
'It is worth something to the rest of us,' said Madge, 'as we are the other kind.'

I must warn those few reading this who do not already admire Miss Compton-Burnett that she is a brainy writer, who touches the heart, and that not often, only by cerebral means. Therefore she should be read when the brain is alert or else her subtleties will be missed, and her writing is entirely interwoven subtleties.

Collected Stories, Sir Osbert Sitwell

Sir Osbert Sitwell says in his preface to *Collected Stories* that novels and short stories have always been his favourite reading. They are clearly his favourite writing, and his own enjoyment comes through to the reader. I think that of all his writing, Sir Osbert will be remembered chiefly for his short stories, and this volume of thirty-three of them is something to buy and keep, not just to borrow. It contains tales which are undoubted masterpieces.

For me the best is 'Low Tide', about two old ladies in Scarborough who lost all their money. Some fools have called this tragic tale heartless, maybe because they are incapable of appreciating the deep pity with which it is imbued. Indeed, it is the author's interest in people which is the interest of these stories.

I do notice, however, that his earlier stories (and they do not seem to be arranged chronologically in this book, so you have to date them by inference) are inspired by pity for the passing of the good manners and established order of pre-1914 society. The later tales are inspired by wrath at the pretentiousness which can pass for merit in the Welfare State.

A splendid satire on this sort of thing is 'The Glow Worm'. It is about a sloppy young journalist who has cashed in on 'kindness', and develops a halo during the war which he cannot conceal in the blackout, and which leads him to well-merited disaster.

***

A Humorous Writer with Suspense and Pathos

Nineteen to the Dozen, Arthur Marshall

24 April 1953

৪০ ७३

Arthur Marshall is for me one of our funniest men. You have probably heard him in the past as Nurse Dugdale or on one of those surprising nature rambles on the wireless, or you have read his descriptions of girls' school stories. There is a tribute to Angela Brazil at the end of *Nineteen to the Dozen*, a collection of his short stories and sketches, which is in this vein. Like all the best humorists, he has a strong sense of pathos.

The stories in this book vary from tragedy to comedy, and sometimes are a knockout mixture of both. He is essentially a writer of the spoken word and the stories read out loud very well. He can create suspense. The funniest suspense is, perhaps, where he describes himself locked in a French 'water' off the rue de Rivoli, and tries to attract attention with varieties of French, idiomatic and classical.

Irony and Satire

The saddest suspense is in a story called 'The Experience', which might be described as an unsentimental version of *Mrs Miniver*. And for satire, I don't think I have read anything today, except some of the works of Wyndham Lewis and Cyril Connolly, which can touch the sustained irony of a little piece called 'Glad to be Back'. It is a patronising, cautious, shamelessly embarrassing address to a soldier returning to his office, delivered by one of the staff who has remained in London through the war.

This remarkable writer is a housemaster at an English public school, and one story called 'File Copies' is a subtle summary of the school careers of two boys told in the form of letters to parents. It is also, by implication, about their home backgrounds. I can understand that Arthur Marshall's peculiar genius is always hit or miss. But there are so many different kinds of stories, about so many different kinds of people, from private soldiers in the war, the officers' mess, American actors and actresses, to schoolgirls and schoolmasters, widows and orphans, in so many moods, that no reader can fail to be impressed by some of the stories. Many will be impressed by all.

Old Wodehouse Spell

Ring for Jeeves, P.G. Wodehouse

A strange thing has happened to P.G. Wodehouse. In *Ring for Jeeves* he dares to insert into the dream world he has created of half-baked peers, millionaires, gentlemen's gentlemen and lovely girls, an acknowledgement of the social revolution. 'You know, Jeeves, even in these disturbed post-war days, with the social revolution turning hand-springs on every side ...' Once one has got over the shock, the old spell reasserts itself.

Bertie Wooster has been put away in some suspiciously vague place and Jeeves, in his master's absence, is butler to Lord Rowcester (pronounced Rooster), who is in a bad way financially — unusual in a Wodehouse peer. Indeed, Lord Rowcester is in such a bad way that he has had to become a bookie, and he takes on a bet which he cannot pay.

He is pursued by an infuriated Capt. Biggar, whose 'eyes were cold and hard, like picnic eggs'. A rich American widow and the peer's sister and her tactless husband, and a pretty young lady vet, and Jeeves himself, take part in an exciting enough story. Though the whole thing is to a formula, one can only admire the sure way in which it is done. In this book I found myself, for the first time for ten years, coming back under the Wodehouse spell which held me when I was a youth.

Casino Thrills

Casino Royale, Ian Fleming

Casino Royale, by Ian Fleming should, I suppose, rightly have been relegated to the reviewer of thrillers. But those who know the sweating excitement of gambling in a casino, the dry shuffle of cards, the intent faces of the gamblers pretending to be bored, and the awful depression of staking everything and losing, will be excited by this spy story for other than the usual thriller reasons.

It is exciting as a gamble, as well as a story of an English secret service agent who is employed to outgamble a Communist agent, who has foolishly been spending his Trade Union funds in a French Casino. It suffers from falling apart two-thirds of the way through, when it becomes a rather physical love story on a different plane from the earlier part of the book.

Ian Fleming has discovered the secret of narrative art — a secret which Nevil Shute told me lately — which is to work up to a climax unrevealed at the end of each chapter. Thus the reader has to go on reading.

A Country House in Norfolk
in Edwardian Days

The Go-Between, L.P. Hartley

9 October 1953

ℬↃↄℬ

O f all the novels L.P. Hartley has written, I think *The Go-Between* is the best. It starts in an unassuming way, almost uninvitingly for hurried people, with its careful recapturing of the atmosphere of a country house in Norfolk in Edwardian days. Here, one feels, is a cultivated voice speaking, in well-chosen words, giving one time to savour what it is saying.

Gradually one finds oneself listening more and more until after the first three or four chapters one finds oneself completely absorbed and dreading that the story will end, because it is so fascinating. Like most really good novels, it is several stories going on at the same time. I do not mean there are a lot of sub-plots, there are none, but that several stories are going on at different levels.

First there is the story itself just as news. Leo Colston, a thirteen-year-old schoolboy, goes to stay with a rather uninteresting but rich and snobbish little school friend of his in Norfolk. Marian Maudsley, the daughter of the house – her father is a rich businessman, her mother a lady of social ambition – is in love with a local farmer, a rough man with a hasty temper and bullish good looks.

Secret Notes

She is about to be engaged to a young peer, disfigured in the Boer War, and a thoroughly nice man, the soul of honour and moreover a man of humour and kindness. Leo is employed to take secret notes between Marian and the farmer and cryptic verbal messages between Marian and the peer. The story works up to a dramatic and searing climax when his errand running is discovered.

Next, there is the emotional development of the boy himself and the effect of these mysterious adult love affairs on his own mind and his relationship with his school friend and the various grown-ups in the house and neighbourhood. Lastly there is the implied relationship between Marian and her lovers and between Marian and her family.

All this is described in the hot sunny leisure of a long ago summer when England was top nation in the world and social distinctions were the very oil of the wheels of life. Mr Hartley never puts a foot wrong in observation or conversation. He never over-analyses, which is the temptation to which duller novelists succumb; he is an artist who knows what to omit. His epilogue, revisiting today the scene of that long-ago tragic scandal, seems to me a perfect conclusion.

This reminds me of the great days of Edwardian novel writing, which suits a story of these times. It is in what's to me the best tradition of fiction.

***

Amusing Story of Life at a Provincial University

Lucky Jim, Kingsley Amis

5 February 1954

଼ଠ୯ଓ

I do not remember to have laughed so much at a new funny book as I have done at *Lucky Jim*, by Kingsley Amis, since when I first read Evelyn Waugh's *Decline and Fall* — and that was in 1928. The scene is a provincial university, an exam-passing, self-important, mercenary world where a good memory was mistaken for learning, where futile essays were written each with 'its funereal parade of yawn-enforcing facts, the pseudo-light it threw on non-problems'.

A good deal of such nonsense goes on at Oxford and Cambridge too in the name of 'research' into history, literature and art. For me, the most refreshing feature of Mr Amis's book is his tolerant contempt for the whole set-up which keeps the reader giggling throughout the book.

His hero, James Dixon, is a lecturer on history, newly arrived and not secure in his position. He is in his probationary first year of teaching and already one of the nastier of his pupils delights in showing up his tutor's ignorance. Chiefly poor Dixon has to keep in with his Professor, a mad mediaevalist who is very musical and gives madrigal concerts with oboes and recorders.

A Madrigal Party

Dixon having disgraced himself at a madrigal party by not being able to sing in tune, escaped from the house where he was staying with his Professor as host and came back drunk. He went to the bathroom to eat toothpaste and try to feel better.

When he woke up next morning he found he had burned huge holes in his bedclothes with a cigarette. He tried to repair the damage by sawing away the burnt fringe with a razor and only made matters worse.

These and similar situations carry one through a book which is itself a good story, full of suspense and with a most satisfying happy ending. Every character is distinct – the lady don with thick spectacles who is in love with Dixon and always making scenes with him; the footling Professor: 'There was a small golden emblem on his tie resembling some heraldic device or other, but proving on close scrutiny to be congealed egg-yoke. Substantial traces of the same nutritive was to be seen round his mouth, which was now ajar.'

There is the Professor's formidable wife, his two ghastly sons and a variety of comic characters, none hated and all lifelike. The one adverse criticism I can make is that there is a certain amount of overwriting but this is wholly outweighed by the merits of the comedy. Indeed, it is a Harold Lloyd film or a Buster Keaton film in prose, lacking the pathos of Chaplin, but with the joyful genius of those other two old stars.

***

Unforgettable Scientific Prophecy

Fahrenheit 451, Ray Bradbury

2 April 1954

৪১ ୯৪

Ray Bradbury, an American, is far the best science fiction writer. But it comes as no surprise to me to find *Fahrenheit 451* a betrayal of modem science and the false idea that 'progress' can be reckoned in terms of scientific inventions. He is too much of a poet in all he writes, too full of imagination to be anything but a prophet.

He foresees an America living in cities and at war with the rest of the world. A war is a matter of sending out flights of bombers and is over in forty-eight hours. All houses are fireproof. Interior walls are huge television screens. Conversation is just mutual back-slapping. Education is just committing facts to memory. No opinions, no philosophy or sociology are allowed. Religion is run by advertising firms and Our Lord is used for toothpaste advertisements.

His hero is a man called Montag, a fireman. Firemen in his world are used to start fires, not to prevent them. They are a sort of sanitary squad and rush out, at the command of the State Police, to burn any secret hoards of books. Books are illegal. One reads from State-selected books thrown on to the television screen.

Montag is so foolish as to steal one of the books from a pile he is burning and to read it. He also makes friends with a young girl who is a rebel and subsequently liquidated. Montag's wife betrays him to the police and he escapes, in a thrilling chase wherein he is pursued by an eight-legged mechanical hound.

I have left out of this description the powerful horror of this unlikeable but compelling tale. I advise it for all worshippers of speed, popular wireless entertainment, luxury flats and mechanical labour-saving devices. Once read it will never be forgotten and should be in every laboratory and technical college and atomic plant in the country — if those places are allowed subversive books.

*****

These Stories are Kind, Catty, Simulating and Subtle

Hester Lilly, Elizabeth Taylor

15 October 1954

ജ‌ൽ

I find the writing of Elizabeth Taylor fresh, and inevitably hitting the right nail on the head in every sentence. It is completely up my street so far as subjects are concerned — ladies in tea shops, sad, forgotten people in public institutions, refined people, vulgar people, Surrey, school common rooms, quarrelling wives and husbands at that critical stage of middle age when the children are beginning to fly the nest and they are left with each other for the rest of their lives. In fact I find her so unbelievably good, kind, stimulating, catty and subtle that I forget I am a critic.

The truth is I can find nothing to complain of in *Hester Lilly* unless it be a slight tendency to let commas do the work of conjunctions, which is a modern trick derived, I think, from Henry James.

Hester Lilly is a short novel about a young woman who is in love with her middle-aged cousin, the married headmaster of a boys' boarding school. She goes to live with him, and the reactions of his wife to her and of the various masters on the school staff to them both, works up to an exciting and ironic conclusion. Even better than *Hester Lilly* are the short stories which take up the second half of the book.

With an understanding which reminds me of Monica Dickens at her best, she can get under the skin of all sorts of unconsidered people. There is a masterly story here called 'Spry Old Character', about an old cockney whose only interest in life was horses and betting and who went blind late in life. On the death of his sister, who had looked after him, he was put into a State institution for the blind.

Here his conversation and personal habits were not refined enough for the other blind people and he found his only outlet in the company of the drivers and conductors down at the bus terminus on the common outside the institution.

Of course the Home for the Blind received the things left over from Harvest Festival, but 'the bread in the shape of a cornsheaf tasted of incense, and with its mainly visual appeal, was wasted on the blind', I could continue quoting Elizabeth Taylor and praising her for the rest of this page.

Lord of the Flies, William Golding

Let no one suppose that, because it is about a party of boys dropped on a deserted tropic island, *Lord of the Flies*, by William Golding, is anything like *Coral Island*. I think it will make entertaining reading for boys, even though the beasts which lurk in the jungle and haunt the lonely starlit nights of the boys are only the creations of the imaginations of the younger boys of the party. But the entertainment that boys and adults will have in this readable and blood-curdling book will be derived from that rather unpalatable thing, the moral which it teaches.

The boys elect as their chief the one among their number who is most sensible and adult and who realises that if they want to be rescued they must keep a smoky fire going. Soon the school bully among them founds his own tribe of hunters and institutes a reign of terror and deposes the elected chief. He works his tribe up to mass blood lust and two of the weaker and more individualistic boys are murdered.

The child is father to the man, if I may be scarcely original. What these boys do to one another is what we as adults do to one another, if we refuse to think of the common good, reverence nothing and obey only our senses.

***

Leonardo of Victorian Era

Isambard Kingdom Brunel: A Biography, L.T.C. Rolt

8 February 1957

ଥ୍ଓ ଓଃ

I sambard Kingdom Brunel was one of the greatest men of the last century or, indeed, of any century in Western Christendom. If he can compare with anyone, he is something like Leonardo da Vinci.

Both were artists and scientists – and if people doubt so seemingly extravagant a claim for a Victorian engineer who worked mostly with cast iron and steam engines, L.T.C. Rolt's inspiring biography will substantiate the claim.

Brunel was born at Portsea in 1806. His father was a French refugee, married to an English woman. This Marc Brunel invented improvements to block-making machinery which had a profound effect on British engineering.

When his son Isambard was eighteen, he was helping him in the construction of the first subaqueous tunnel in the world, which runs under the Thames from Wapping to Rotherhithe. To this day its brick arches may be seen by anyone who stands on Wapping Underground Station and looks down the railway tunnel that it has now become.

When he was twenty-four, I.K. Brunel won the competition for the suspension bridge at Clifton, beating even the veteran engineer Telford with his design. This superbly elegant structure was completed after his death by Sir John Hawkshaw, as a memorial to his genius.

Brunel's Intrepidity

It is characteristic of the intrepidity of Brunel that, when work started on the bridge and an iron bar was stretched across the deep abyss of the Avon Gorge, he should make the first journey across it in a basket suspended from a pulley. Halfway across the roller stuck, and breathless workmen on either bank saw the young engineer climb up the rope and free the roller.

His next work was what he regarded as his greatest — the construction of the Great Western Railway from Bristol to Paddington. This involved the making of the box tunnel and in 1838 the construction of the beautiful brick railway bridge over the Thames at Maidenhead which consists of two of the largest and flattest arches that had ever been built in brickwork. Everyone prophesied they would collapse, but there they are to this day, and Brunel's bridge makes even the elegant eighteenth-century road bridge adjacent to it look commonplace.

Metal and Glass

The bridges at Saltash and Chepstow are two more familiar examples of his genius. In 1850 he rebuilt Paddington Station entirely of metal and glass and, since it is in a cutting, with no exterior walls.

What his rival and friend Robert Stephenson was to the North and the narrower gauge railways, Brunel was to the West with his broad gauge. These were the days when Bristol was losing its trade to Liverpool, and it was this rivalry which gave Brunel the opportunity to design the first large steamship to cross the Atlantic, in an attempt to bring back ocean trade to Bristol.

His death was precipitated by the disgusting trickery, swindling and denigration he suffered from a jealous megalomaniac engineer called Scott Russell over the building of the *Great Eastern* steamship. Brunel died aged fifty-two, and never saw his great vessel sail.

Like his predecessor Telford, he was an artist and architect. But he was a more original architect than Telford, as all who have seen the interesting Telford Exhibition in London will know when they compare Telford's architecture with Brunel's.

We can see the trouble he took over the Italianate pumping stations for the now defunct atmospheric railway from Exeter to Dawlish, over the Egyptian-shaped piers at Clifton Bridge and the tunnel openings, viaducts and stations, where these survive unmolested, on the Great Western. His diaries record his delight in visiting cathedrals. Architecture and engineering to Brunel were one.

Mr Rolt has the rare gift of making the technical problems of engineering interesting and comprehensible to the layman. He combines with this an appreciation of Brunel's forthright, vigorous and humorous character. When complaining of the refreshment rooms at Swindon, Brunel wrote that: 'Mr Player was wrong in supposing that I thought you purchased inferior coffee. I thought I said to him I was surprised you should buy such bad roasted corn. I did not believe you had such a thing as coffee in the place.'

We learn of how, when Brunel was nearly choking to death through swallowing a half-sovereign while doing conjuring tricks for his children, he invented a revolving board on to which he was strapped down, whirled round and eventually delivered of the half-sovereign through his mouth.

I can think of few people I would sooner have met than this man Mr Rolt has so well presented to us. I would like to know more about how he stands in relation to other engineers of his time and to Victorian society in general.

The publishers should have been more generous with their illustrations, and might have made the format of the book look much less like a textbook for students.

***

'About a Novelist Going Mad'

The Ordeal of Gilbert Pinfold, Evelyn Waugh

19 July 1957

ꔫ

When somebody asked Evelyn Waugh what his new novel was about he is said to have answered: 'About a middle-aged Roman Catholic novelist going mad.' And here is *The Ordeal of Gilbert Pinfold*.

Pinfold is a middle-aged writer with a wife and large family who lives in the country in the style of a gentleman of pre-1914 days. He feels a little cut off from neighbours and some of his friends because he is a Roman Catholic.

He dislikes the wireless and people it employs, Picasso, plastics, sunbathing and jazz — 'everything in fact that had happened in his own life-time'. He dislikes intrusions on his privacy. He loves his wife and children and those of his old friends who do not perform on the wireless. He is under the impression that he is fundamentally amiable and gentlemanly. He begins to hear voices and suffer from delusions. To escape them he takes a sea voyage alone. The ship seems to him to be haunted. He hears all the sorts of people he doesn't like conspiring to persecute him. He hears his most intimate shames discussed.

Now and then — and this is the most skilful thing about this cleverly constructed book — he becomes sane enough to see the captain of the ship and his fellow passengers for what they really are, decent middle-class rather boring Britons.

Then we are back into schoolboy persecution with all the mean and wounding things that were said to us as our enemies gathered round in the playground, translated into adult terms. Towards the end of the book Mr Pinfold suffers from the common delusion in the advance of madness that he is a wireless set receiving messages from his enemies in a far country. I have had letters from such people.

I ask myself 'Is this novel autobiography?' It is certainly a picture of hell on earth. It is not a picture of madness but of the stages leading to it. I have an idea that most of us are haunted by voices such as these.

I know that in times of depression I hear arguments such as Mr Waugh describes going on in my head; indeed, in moments of searing self-examination I discover what I am really like underneath through the medium of these arguments which expose one's secret shames. The picture is most unpleasant. I would say that the ordeal of Gilbert Pinfold is self-examination written as a novel but unlike other such works, which are generally dreary and self-pitying, this, because it is by Mr Waugh, is readable, thrilling and detached.

What is it that makes Mr Waugh so good a writer? Is it just his careful use of grammar and punctuation, narrative power, conciseness and Firbankian gift for the unexpected? I think it is more than these. It is something which comes in from outside — that is genius.

The Called and the Chosen, Monica Baldwin

If those who read Monica Baldwin's *The Called and the Chosen* think they are in for another autobiography like her *I Leap Over the Wall*, they are right. But this time she has written the story of a nun who is not Miss Baldwin, but someone else.

Her nun, who writes in the first person, is brought up by a pious aunt, who destines her for the Roman Church. She lives in a beautiful house in England which has belonged to her family since the reign of Henry VIII, and she is the last of the line.

Her aunt puts her into a Belgian convent where all the time she finds herself thinking about her home in England and how she longs to be back there. When the war comes and her aunt dies, the Belgian community is left this country house.

The nun returns and in agony watches the family heirlooms sold, the garden and trees cut down, the glorious painted dining room whitewashed and turned into a chapel, the chimney pieces and pictures taken away and the house treated with that disregard for aesthetic beauty known only to the truly spiritual.

How she reconciles herself to the return of her house in this manner to the church from which she thinks her ancestors received it from the hands of Henry VIII is the main theme of the book. It is extremely well told and full of humour; from it one learns how nuns can be just as odious to one another as those of us are who live in the world.

The book is at once a warning to those who imagine that to join a convent or monastery is to escape from responsibilities and — what is more remarkable — a pointer to the immense rewards which the sacrifice of life in the world to life with God can bring. It is Miss Baldwin's gift that she can hint at heavenly joy. It is not Mr Waugh's gift. The mental torture Miss Baldwin's nun suffers is a deeper, though less painful agony than that of Mr Pinfold.

***

Response to Revelation

2 July 1972

The Faber Book of Religious Verse

৪০ ৫৪

This anthology much impresses me. Its editor, Helen Gardner, is deeply read in English poetry from Anglo-Saxon times to the present day. She is an unshowy scholar who has not caught foot-and-note disease. Those notes she does provide are short, clear and necessary. She considers that a religious poem is concerned 'in some way with revelation and man's response to it'. Religious poems need not be Christian, though this anthology containing English and Welsh poets (and two Scottish and two Irish) is mainly of Christian poetry.

What poetry is, I do not quite know. Maybe it is the right words in the right order. For me it requires rhythm and, as an extra flourish, rhyme. It is the shortest and the most memorable way of saying what you want said.

The Faber Book of Religious Verse is welcome because it is a distillation of distillations. Dame Helen's definition of a religious poem enables her to include Shelley's 'Hymn to Intellectual Beauty' and parts of 'Adonais'. Shelley's awareness of 'the awful shadow of some unseen Power' makes him a religious poet. For the same reason Emily Brontë's 'God of Visions' is included. These abstractions are strange company for tender adorers of Our Lady in mediaeval English poetry and for friendly old Calvinists like Isaac Watts who rightly appear in this book. She has also included, as religious poetry, full-blooded satires on hypocrites of which the best until now is Robert Burns's 'Holy Willie's Prayer'.

Palgrave's *Golden Treasury*, which to me is still the best anthology of English poetry, was edited to be read from beginning to end as a biography. It travels from youth to age, from spring to winter and from mood to mood, with stimulating subtlety. Dame Helen's anthology is concerned with what is *outside* time. The poets are arranged chronologically, but this book also can be read from beginning to end as though it were a novel or a biography. First comes an unknown tenth-century Anglo-Saxon poet who makes the Cross which carried a triumphant Lord speak to the people in the wood-walled nave below:

> Hope sprang up again
> Bright with blessing to those burning in pain
> Christ the Son of God journeyed as a Conqueror
> Mighty and Victorious, when with many in his train.
> A great company of souls, he came to God's Kingdom —
> The one Almighty to the bliss of the angels
> And of all the holy ones who in heavenly places
> Abode in glory — when Almighty God,
> The King of Kings, came home, to his own country.

In this translation, by Dame Helen herself, there if much in common with the Christ of David Gascoyne's 'Ecce Homo' (1916):

> Not from a monstrance silver-wrought
> But from the tree of human pain
> Redeem our sterile misery,
> Christ of Revolution and of Poetry,
> That man's long journey through the night
> May not have been in vain.

The 'pious English' were known for their devotion to Our Lady. Stained-glass windows in cathedrals and college chapels display that devotion right through the Renaissance — the blue-robed Virgin and the golden nimbus:

> Now goeth sun under wood —
> Me rueth, Mary, thy fair rode.

Now goeth sun under tree —
Me rueth, Mary, thy son and thee.

'Me rueth' means 'I grieve for' and 'the rode' is 'the cross'. It is not unlike the Auden of 1945 in 'For the time being':

Dream. In human dreams earth ascends to Heaven
Where no one need pray nor ever feel alone.
In your first few hours of life here, O have you
Chosen already what death must be your own?
How soon will you start on the Sorrowful Way?
Dream while you may.

Surprisingly the time when the Church was supposed to be dead, the eighteenth century, produces some of the most magnificent religious poetry. In Christopher Smart's 'Song to David' with its stupendous climax, Cowper's hymns, Blake's lyrics and best of all Charles Wesley's 'Wrestling Jacob'. His is a colloquy with God as love:

Yield to me now — for I am weak;
But confident in self-despair:
Speak to my heart, in blessings speak,
Be conquered by my instant prayer,
Speak, or thou never hence shalt move,
And tell me, if thy name is love.

I miss, in the last century, Keble's plain sense and Bishop Heber's exotic lyrics. The power of both these as poets still comes through their words, however familiar the tunes to which we sing them.

His monthly causerie

about buildings ancient and modern

Men and Buildings

ഇൻ ൽ

Launched on 10 March 1958, 'Men and Buildings' would appear every four weeks, always on a Monday on the features pages, and over six and a half years provided Betjeman with a regular architectural platform in the *Telegraph*, one he grasped with some gusto. The column looked at architecture in a more holistic way than was generally the case previously (for example 'Architecture is not just building. It is also gardens and trees in which buildings are set') and would happily take in street furniture, gardens, vernacular buildings, townscapes or anything else that took Betjeman's fancy. Victorian buildings clearly did, modern developers all too often did not. So informed, wide-ranging and generally interesting on its subject is this series that it could easily justify an entire book of its own, even if at times the same complaints about unsympathetic new buildings and developments do string across the articles a bit too over-regularly. Alas space permits just a selection, so here are those which, for me, best encapsulate this stimulating series.

Country House Heritage

7 April 1958

ဣၩႏ

Country houses are part of the English landscape. Georgian and Victorian squires planted the woods around them which we enjoy today. Yet the complete village, with its big house still in good repair and lived in by the family which built it; its church served by its own vicar, its cottages, new and old, built of local material and inhabited – such a complete unit is now almost unknown.

But how well one knows the feel of the presence of a big house – the planted woods which adorn the hills, the high park wall, the lodges and gates, the avenues sweeping away to hidden private splendour, the lake, the fishponds, the ice-house, the sheltered kitchen garden, the folly on the hill, the stable clock chiming over the yard a full five minutes ahead of the church clock in the village, the hunters in the paddock, the estate cottages deep in their well-worked gardens of fruit and vegetables and flowers, the neatly ordered farms and snug stack-yards, the family arms on hatchments in the church and swinging on a sign over the village inn.

Today the woods are down, ruined Army huts deface the park, the gates are sold, the park wall has fallen, the church is locked. The village is strung with poles and wires, and most of it has been rebuilt to look as much like Slough as possible, the kitchen garden has been ploughed, the folly has disappeared, demolishers have bought all the chimney pieces and panelling of the old house and these, like its pictures and furniture, have either been sold to America or gone to adorn the board rooms of investment trusts. And you and I are labelled Tories for not regarding this as progress.

Why Not Here?

Most European countries, whatever their politics, have kept their country houses intact, realising that they are an asset not just to tourists but to their own peoples. Most of the great English architects, from Tudor times down to Norman Shaw and Sir Edwin Lutyens, were employed to design country houses in all the varied styles and materials which make the English landscape so beautiful and exciting with its constant change. Here are five reasons why we should preserve our remaining country houses.

First, there are comparatively few of them. I believe Mr James Lees-Milne, the architectural adviser on buildings to the National Trust, once calculated that there were 323 country houses of 'historic and architectural interest' in England and Wales. Since the war 153 country houses (not all on that list) have been demolished. They therefore have a rarity value. They are irreplaceable, as no one could afford to build a large country house today, I should think the last to be built was Gladstone Hall, near Skipton, Yorkshire, which was designed for a mill owner, Sir Amos Nelson, in 1920 by Lutyens.

Secondly, they are beautiful buildings in themselves, and, like much English architecture, very often grander within than their modest exteriors would lead you to suppose. Sometimes they were built all at once: more often they are the gradual growth of centuries, but not so many centuries, for the period of country house building is quite a short one even in our recorded history. Except for a few old castles and manor houses it began in Tudor times and ended with the present century.

My third reason is that the country house itself is only part of its effect. The trees in the park, the lakes, temples, stable block and church and village are all an essential part of its architecture, because England is, or rather was, above everything, a landscape garden famous throughout the world.

Fourthly, country houses are the homes of people who may have lived there for generations, whose children grew up in the village and knew the village people. For instance, the Giffards have lived at Chillington Hall, Staffs, since 1178.

English landlords have been on the whole benevolent and not absentees. They are generally regarded with affection by their tenants. The portraits in a country house are much more alive when you can see the house in which the persons depicted lived, the monuments to them in the neighbouring church and the improvements this or that owner made. And we all know that furniture in a house which is used is preferable to dead specimens in a museum.

Lastly, we who live in small houses and the roar of towns need the sense of permanence and tranquillity which country houses give. It is sentimental to assume that because we live in an industrial age on wheels that the life of a country gentleman is therefore an anachronism which should be abolished. Just because we live in noise and speed and constant change what remains on this island of quietude, slowness and permanence becomes increasingly precious.

Last Defences

Between the merciless tax collector with his assistants the demolishers and auctioneers and those few country houses that remain there stand a few vigorous defences which need all the support we can give.

There is the National Trust, which is not a government department but a voluntary organisation kept going by subscriptions from all who value tranquillity and permanence. The National Trust owns 130 country houses which have been handed over by their owners with a capital sum to provide income for upkeep. The Trust makes up the deficit.

About 160 country houses besides these are open to the public. Some are in government ownership. Organisations like the Cheshire Foundation and the Mutual Households Association have taken on large old houses; the Cheshire Foundation is for the sick, and the Mutual Households Association is for retired people who want a self-contained flat in a country house with communal dining.

Local councils have sometimes saved a house. The Swindon Corporation set a fine example by buying and preserving Lydiard Tregoze, where the Lords Bolingbroke lived. Some palatial houses like Chatsworth, Burghley, Longleat and Woburn are helped by visitors' entrance fees, but the lesser country houses, in their gentle way just as beautiful, stand little chance of survival unless something is done to enable their owners to live in them.

The admirable Historic Buildings Council makes grants towards the repairs of houses of architectural merit and this grant comes from a government vote of £400,000 a year. But this sum goes towards other buildings as well as country houses, and is not designed to provide an income for the luckless owner of a country house which he and his family have loved for generations. It merely helps to repair his walls and roof. Today it is a crime to be a country gentleman, and the smaller English country houses will soon all disappear.

***

Muddle on the Roads

2 June 1958

ಬಂಡಿ

Roads in Britain are exempt from planning. When you think of the thousands of miles of roads there are and how small is our island and how delicate and varied its scenery, this is formidable.

The chief people responsible for roads are the Minister of Transport and the engineers of the local authorities through which the roads pass. The Ministry of Transport and the local authority engineers, with very few exceptions, think of roads entirely in terms of traffic and cash. They want to put up as many signs, poles and lamp standards as they can to make things easy for the motorist, and they want to do it as cheaply as possible.

The Ministry issues a thick and puzzling catalogue of hundreds of compulsory and optional signs, of designs which the Ministry imposes – those huge direction boards on a yellow background for long distances and blue for local, attached to iron supports by nuts and bolts at the back; the 'Keep Left' bollards, the 'Halt', 'School', 'Level Crossing' and other signs: traffic lights and their switch gear, and parking notices.

Outmoded Lighting

The Borough Engineer chooses the lamp standards and the kind of light which is to flood the road. He generally sticks to the ugly patterns which are now out of date because the order was placed for them before local objections to their hideousness were made, and he cannot cancel his order without incurring 'unnecessary expense' and losing face.

For the same reason he feels himself obliged to stick to the sort of lighting he originally ordered, let us say sodium, though the adjacent borough has mercury lighting. Neither he nor his neighbouring borough can have recourse to the new colour-corrected mercury which gives a less offensive light and does not require either a pig trough or a luncheon basket at the top of the standard to display it, but can be introduced to well-designed lamp-posts, old or new.

The Ministry of Transport compels the local engineer to use 25-foot columns 120 feet apart on class A roads and 15-foot columns on side roads. The standards are erected strictly according to rule, regardless of the buildings or trees beside them.

New Technique

Sometimes the Royal Fine Art Commission has been called in by local inhabitants, and in the exceptional case of Marlborough the Minister of Transport allowed a certain relaxation of the rules.

With new developments in lighting technique it is possible to use standards 35 or 40-feet-high spaced at about 300 feet, instead of the 120 feet spacing with 25-foot standards. This reduces the forest of columns, and would be more in scale with most redevelopment in large urban areas.

The Sanitary Engineer erects his notices – 'Men' and 'Women', 'Ladies' and 'Gents', 'Lavatory' or 'Convenience', according to the social status of the area. The transport authority (in London the London Transport Executive) erects bus shelters, bus stops, trolley bus standards. The Post Office erects telephone kiosks and letter boxes. The RAC, the AA, the Services and various big contractors introduce their own temporary direction signs. The police erect kiosks, street telephones and temporary notices.

Down country lanes and through villages, the poles of the Post Office and Electricity Board march side by side. The road surface engineer introduces directions in white paint on the surface and adds concrete verges. The railways have their signs pointing to stations, and as a sop to 'amenities' the Borough Engineer plants a rockery in the middle of an island which no one can reach without endangering his life, and plants flowers on it which no one can see or smell for the passage of traffic and the fumes of petrol. And here and there the local council may set down a litter basket and bench for contemplation of what has become the most untidy, strident muddle in our island – the public road.

Claims of Grace

But roads are not designed solely for motorists. All of us walk along streets as well as drive down them. Space and grace are as worthy of consideration as traffic and cash. Famous thoroughfares such as

Grey Street, Newcastle upon Tyne, the High at Oxford, Burford High Street, Hamilton Square, Birkenhead, the streets of Ludlow, Louth, Stamford and other glorious towns are all at the mercy of the local engineer and the Ministry of Transport, whose rules are sightlessly carried out to the letter (so as to obtain a grant).

Only in the New Towns and in Coventry and, just lately, in London and in the small market town of Faringdon have Borough Engineers started to work with architects and planning officers. Until all roads, by Act of Parliament, are put under overall control of a single authority – and he should be the County Planning Officer – the confusing litter of signs on our highways will grow. Our road scenery is at the mercy of so many autonomous authorities which are not concerned about anything except traffic and cheapness.

***

Heritage of the Rail Age

8 February 1960

ಬಾ ಲ

The LCC has given permission to British Railways to demolish the Great Arch at Euston, and its attendant lodges. It has made the wise condition 'provided that they are re-erected on another site in an appropriate, dignified and open setting'.

The Arch was completed in 1837 from designs by Philip Hardwick and marked the arrival of the railway from Birmingham to London. It was a symbolic gateway heralding the new mode of transport and built with all the courage and swagger of a time which was convinced of a glorious future.

Its enormous granite blocks have withstood the London atmosphere, its proportions are vast and awe-inspiring and are given scale by the attendant lodges and railings. It was intended to be seen from the Euston Road but has since been obscured by an hotel and its lodges have been defaced by additions to the station.

I can think of no worthier memorial to the fact that Britain built the first railways than to reconstruct this Arch, its lodges and railings on the Euston Road itself.

Decaying Splendour

Railways were born in England. The early railway architecture of this country is therefore of more than merely national importance. It is the beginning of the whole history of the Railway Age.

If it were just *old*, I would not be so anxious to plead for its preservation. It is also often very fine, particularly in its stations, viaducts, bridges and tunnel entrances.

Large cast-iron roofs such as those at St Pancras and York Central are still among the engineering wonders of the world. The wooden roof of the original station at Temple Meads, Bristol, has a span exceeding that of Westminster Hall, the largest mediaeval wooden roof in existence. Not only for their engineering feats are the railways of the United Kingdom remarkable, but also for the architecture of their stations.

Unfortunately railway enthusiasts are mostly people interested in engines and speeds of trains and the history of railway development. There is very little written about railway buildings. The names of the architects of some of our grandest stations such as Temple Meads are forgotten.

Partly because of this and partly because of an incredible insensitivity to architecture on the part of the British Transport Commission in the past, a great many splendid buildings have been mutilated or allowed to decay.

Since the war, for instance, one of the earliest railway stations in the world, that at Nine Elms, Vauxhall, London (1837–8), with its arcaded entrance, has been partly demolished. The vista Brunel designed for Paddington Station, the only large London building with no exterior walls, has been obscured by a new and needless screen at the platform barriers. The roof of Edward Middleton Barry's railway hotel at Charing Cross with its mansard roof and spikes, so pleasant and prominent a feature of the Strand and Thames skyline, has been flattened and reconstructed in a feeble semi-Georgian manner.

The magnificent Cannon Street awaits no doubt a similar fate, with its enclosing walls now open to the sky. The tower top which lent unity to the buildings of Liverpool Street has been removed. Unworthy electric light fittings have been clamped haphazardly on to the brickwork of St Pancras Station entrances. Holborn Viaduct, with its distinguished arcaded entrance and tiled refreshment room, is being destroyed. These examples come from London alone.

Stately Stations

The history of railway stations is in itself interesting. The very first, of which Euston is an example, had arched entrances for road traffic which led to cast-iron sheds over the platforms. Later, protection for the passengers was demanded and a great hall, like the concourse in a modern airport, was constructed in which they could wait until a man came in and rang a bell to announce the departure of a train.

The finest of these survives, again at Euston. It was designed by Philip Hardwick and his son P.C. Hardwick ten years after the Arch and was rightly described by the late H.S. Goodhart-Rendel as 'one of the noblest rooms in London'. Two other grand early stations come to my mind – that at Huddersfield (1850–54), by J. and C. Pritchett, which is like an enormous classical country house with central portico and arcades and wings on either side, and Central Station, Newcastle upon Tyne (1846–9), with its impressive classical entrance by J. Dobson.

The next phase in station development was for an hotel to be built as part of the station. The first was at York and one of the best to survive much as it was originally designed by T. G. Andrews (1847) is that at Paragon Station, Kingston upon Hull, in the Italianate manner.

The first railway stations to be built alongside the line between termini were thought of as lodge gates or tollhouses beside the iron road and were consequently in a cottage style. Many survive, notably in the neighbourhood of Derby. They were generally of local materials and harmonise well with their setting. South London and Surrey have several.

Stations are by no means the only good architecture with which the railways provided Britain. There are bridges – the Britannia Bridge over the Menai Strait, by Robert Stephenson and Francis Thompson (1845–50), with its enormous guardian lions and cyclopean piers and entrances; Conway Bridge in the Gothic style by the same architects, blending with the castle; Brunel's wonderful brick bridge over the Thames at Maidenhead with its nearly flat arches.

Shoddy Treatment

There are viaducts like the Wharncliff Viaduct at Hanwell, Middlesex, and that which carries the London and North Western northwards from Wolverton and those which carry the Midland through Rutland and Northants.

The railways were built by people who were proud of them and thought of their stations, bridges, viaducts and tunnel entrances as the additions to the landscape we now recognise them to be. Their present shoddy treatment is thus doubly distressing.

Pleasant, flimsy wayside stations of wood are allowed to rot and are then replaced with a less functional and infinitely more uncomfortable concrete, so that they are like cold public lavatories.

If ruined castles, decaying churches and country houses are part of our heritage worthy of preservation, so are many of the constructions of our railways. I hope that a survey will be made of our railway architecture and that its best examples will be preserved.

***

Contemporary Without Conscience

7 March 1960

ഇ൪ങ

There are nearly 20,000 architects on the register of the Royal Institute. They cannot all be artists, although architecture is an art.

Some think of themselves as planners. They are concerned how to fit a given number of people into a given space, for a given sum of money. Some have lapsed into the role of public relations officer and are employed to charm committees, overcome obstructions from government departments and local authorities or to take potential clients out to lunch.

Of the architects who design buildings and in person supervise their erection, there are a variety of types. A small and increasingly valuable number of these specialise in the repair of old buildings. Others are doctrinaire advocates of a particular style. Still more will run up for you whatever you want. These employ men to produce flash perspectives to impress customers.

True Artists

There are some who let their buildings speak for themselves. They know that no photograph or smartly rendered perspective or even expensive model really shows you what a building is like. These are the true artists. They think in three-dimensional terms: walk about the building in their minds outside and in before it is built; visualise it in its setting.

They know what they want, and like artists they will not be deflected by outside opinions and current fashions. They have that innate sense of proportion which gives them humour and which cannot be defined even by mathematical rules.

It is only by constantly looking at buildings that you can tell which are works of art and which are not. For instance, why is the modern front by Sir Aston Webb of Buckingham Palace rather dull? And why is the eighteenth-century front of Somerset House on the River Thames by Sir William Chambers so impressive? Both are classical and of Portland stone. Why is Bath Abbey less uplifting than the interior of St Mary Redcliffe, Bristol? Both are in the English Perpendicular style and of nearly similar date. The answer is in the designer.

Derived Ideas

So it is with what has come to be called 'Contemporary'. It is an easy style for the indifferent artist to copy. He can get the parts out of a catalogue and his building can look to the unobservant as impressive as something by a real artist in that style, but it will grow out of date. Great architecture is dateless.

The conscienceless architect knows in his heart that it will be cheaper if the building is not very high to build it with bearing walls, wooden window frames and a pitched roof. But he knows that he has a committee to please and committees are terrified of not being thought up to date, so he makes something in copybook contemporary based on a building in America or Scandinavia or France or in a magazine.

Nothing must be in the centre of anything else. Pillars must have no capitals and be placed not quite flush with what they must support. There must be 'floor-scaping' with pebbles and concrete basins for flowers. On the side of the building there must be a space left for some imitation Henry Moore sculpture done by someone in the local art school. Windows must be set in a frame of concrete projecting beyond the glass. The walls must be of glass, too, brightened with standard primary colours. Lower down variety can be introduced by mosaics. The ground floor must be one sheet of plate glass.

The skyline must be made 'interesting' by either collapsed organ bellows, oval hat boxes or empty pergolas. To show that our age is full of courage the building must be out of all proportion to its neighbours.

More than Style

This rather self-conscious 'being different' can sometimes be brought off by an architect who is a real artist. We know there are not thousands of genuine artists and it is unlikely they will be found in the office of the borough surveyor, the architectural department of a chain store or the big firm which is simply out for money.

Admittedly neo-Georgian could be as comically treated as copybook contemporary, but I have chosen to pillory the latter because it is about time people thought of building as architecture and not simply as style.

***

Restoration has its Limits

4 April 1960

℘ ℭ

If the new does not fully re-create the old, it is perhaps because times have changed for the craftsman too.

Hundreds of thousands of pounds are being spent on refacing the outsides of the older Oxford colleges. Oxford has the same problem as any other city, village or town whose walls the centuries have eroded.

When we have entirely refaced an old building with new material, copying with mechanical exactitude engravings or even the architects' original drawings, if they survive, is the result the same as the building we knew before?

Our eyes and heart tell us no. The result is a plaster cast and not the original. Yet why is this difference, subtle and slight as it is, so disturbingly profound?

For some reason the life goes out of the architecture. This is particularly true of carving, whether it is a Gothic gargoyle, a Renaissance cherub or a swag of stone fruit.

We can all tell at a glance a Victorian building in the mediaeval style just as we know from looking at it that the North Transept entrance of Westminster Abbey by which most visitors enter is largely Victorian stonework. So the Oxford colleges are beginning to look externally at any rate as though they were built today.

At Best a Copy

'But we have the exact design,' the expert will tell you. 'We have an original engraving which shows it as it was.' Or, 'We have an old photograph which shows that piece of sculpture before it had decayed so much as it has done recently. Our new replacement is much more like what the sculptor intended than that broken piece of stone you used to know.'

Only in a sense, and a superficial one, is this true. In the old carving our imagination supplied the missing pieces and continued the flow of the lines which time had obliterated from the sculptor's work. The replacement is at best a skilful copy and has filled in the gaps which our imagination used to fill. It may well be that the copyist did not have the same imagination as either us or the original craftsman.

I think one reason why the new carving is dead is because the original artist worked in different conditions and had an entirely different mind.

If he was a mediaeval carver he lived in Christendom. He believed the unseen world was very near his own. Wolves and fabulous beasts lived in the thick woods around his village. Roads were rough grass tracks. Witches cast spells. Nature pressed in on all sides. God and His Mother seemed near.

If he were a Renaissance carver he had probably never been to Italy and his interpretation of classical themes had an English look. His cherubs were local infants, his fruit was the exotic product of his imagination like those huge pomegranates one sees split open in a tapestry. He had probably never seen a pomegranate. He worked from verbal descriptions. His life was 'nasty, brutish and short'. Hanging, the stocks and the pillory were common public sights.

Can the modern craftsman, clocking in at regular hours, bicycling back to his home and the evening paper and the television, have the same imagination as the sculptor whose work he thinks he is copying so exactly?

I ask this question in particular about some famous bearded gentlemen who stand on pedestals in a semi-circle in front of the Sheldonian Theatre and the old Ashmolean Museum in Broad Street, Oxford. Today they look like illustrations in a medical textbook on skin diseases. No one knows what was the original appearance of these faceless but familiar creatures.

Should they be replaced by recognisable portraits of famous Oxford characters sculptured by a Royal Academician? Should an abstract sculptor supply shapes which would look well in that setting or should they be left as they are, until they have finally withered to nothing?

Change of Texture

As for the old buildings requiring refacement, there is another cause for lifelessness in a new surface and that is the change of texture. The old quarries at Headington and in the Cotswolds from which the Oxford colleges were built are worked out or disused.

It so happens that the human eye is particularly sensitive to the look of textures and we can all distinguish between a plaster cast and an original, between cement and a stone even if it is of the same colour. The stone with which the Oxford colleges are being refaced is not from the old quarries. We can all perceive this.

Add to this the additional texture which time gives to a building. The old and unrestored building may be so weathered that it has ceased to be like what it was originally. Weathered as it is, it is still more recognisably the original building than it will be when it is refaced. It is like a lady who has grown old and shrunken, but has resisted the temptation to have her face lifted.

Or take the analogy of a teddy bear worn with affection. Kind parents may give its owner a new bear of exactly the same shape and nearly the same colour but it will not be the old loved object. It is not merely sentimental to like a building which is weathered and decayed. We have known it in that state all our lives and it is part of us.

I am not writing against restoration. The Oxford college buildings still perform their internal functions admirably. Inside they still have the worn texture of the ages.

I am asking for a more sensitive restoration of their exteriors such as we now make of our old parish churches. This can never be done by a building firm only, working on the instructions of a committee. It must be done by an architect who is an artist in old buildings.

Much better if the walls are not actually letting in the wind and rain to leave them in their present state of decay and concentrate on preserving their surfaces as they are. I would even prefer to see the old stone gentlemen kept in their present sightless contemplation of the New Bodleian.

***

Town Halls Through the Ages

30 May 1960

ଈଓ ଔଓ

O ne day someone will write a book about town halls. Until it appears, here are some dangerous generalisations on them.

They are important chiefly, though not exclusively, in Northern Europe where mayors and burgesses, though often slightly comic, are regarded with the respect we pay to commerce.

Town halls originate from churches. First the nave and church porch were where people met to discuss parish business. Then the trade guilds, and in England particularly those connected with wool, built their own chapels on to the parish church and had their own priests and services.

Over the Market

Later they built themselves a separate hall for conducting business. The Guildhalls of London (1411) and Exeter (1468 and 1594) are surviving witnesses of them.

They do not compare in architectural splendour of late Gothic and early Renaissance with the *hôtels de ville* of France and Belgium. But all over England, particularly in East Anglia and Kent, are cloth halls and guildhalls, the latter usually modest half-timber constructions above an open market like the one at Thaxted, Essex.

Today a town hall is little more than a huge block of offices, with a council chamber hidden away in it somewhere.

The earliest town halls of the seventeenth century imitated the construction, but not the style, of the old guildhalls. They were built on stone pillars over a covered market; Berkshire has typical modest examples in Windsor, Wallingford and Faringdon, and a fine shire hall at Abingdon.

The most elegant Georgian town hall I know is that of High Wycombe (1757), and there is another, rather later, hall built on the same pattern over the market, at Uxbridge. Both are threatened with destruction.

By the end of the eighteenth century mayors and local government had become important enough for the Town Hall to be a separate building from the market. The most handsome building of this period and sort is that at Liverpool by John Wood and Son of Bath.

After the reform of local government in 1832–5, town halls, particularly in the industrial North, began to show the 'brass' and prosperity of local trade. They were to be more palatial inside than the houses of the big landowners who had hitherto dominated local government. Cuthbert Brodrick's Town Hall of Leeds (1853) in its Roman grandeur set an example to all the land.

It was inevitable that some corporations should insist on their ancient origin, discarding the classic for the mediaeval style. Manchester Town Hall (1869), by Alfred Waterhouse, is the grandest example: it is skilfully planned on a triangular site.

Waterhouse believed that you should make your plan first, then draw your skyline, and after that fill in. His great black building with its varied façades, considered outline, and many interior vistas, is still one of the wonders of the North.

Preston Town Hall (1862) by Sir Gilbert Scott – shorn of its clock tower by fire, and now to make way for commerce – and the Town Halls of Northampton (1864) and Congleton (1864), both by E.W. Godwin, are its predecessors.

Oxford's Daring

In the seventies, more house-like buildings in a Jacobean style were considered suitable for secular authorities. Wakefield Town Hall by T.E. Colcutt is one of the best; that at Leicester (1875) by F.J. Hames is another. But the best in this style is Oxford Town Hall

(1892) by Henry T. Hare, in his own exuberant version of early Renaissance. It is a more daring and carefully detailed building than any of the university erections of that time.

At the end of the last century, the mayor and Corporation went in for palaces that were halfway between an hotel and a bank, with towers and domes added to show their importance. Portsmouth Town Hall (1886) by W. Hill is an early example. This period gave us the best Town Hall in the United Kingdom: that of Cardiff (1897) by Lanchester, Stewart and Rickards.

The last named was the only English architect who could design in a true Continental baroque manner. He and his firm were also responsible for the exquisite Town Hall at Deptford (1902) with its decorations recalling the shipbuilding origin of the borough and its golden galleon sailing over the dreary waste of New Cross.

A town hall is now being built in Kensington from the designs of E. Vincent Harris, one of the last men to build in the old classic manner. There were complaints about the style of the design when it was first made public.

Now I see the building itself, the pleasantly low scale it keeps with its surroundings, its handsome massing and thoughtful use of brick and stone, and its strong mouldings, I wonder whether it is not more suitable for municipal pomp than the more clinical style of today. Ermine and red robes do not go with steel chairs and austerity.

If we are still to keep mayors and their dignity perhaps it is as well to set them in architecture suited to their state. This does not, however, justify making the rate collectors' and borough surveyors' offices into palaces.

Towers of Babel

Today, if he had not died at the Council table of the Royal Academy in 1880, would have been the 130th birthday of Edward M. Barry, the architect who completed the work of his father, Sir Charles, on the Houses of Parliament and Halifax Town Hall.

He reconstructed Covent Garden Opera House in the form we know it now and designed the railway stations and hotels of Charing Cross and Cannon Street, so cruelly mutilated by the British Transport Commission. He designed Crewe Hall, Cheshire, the work in which he took the greatest pride, and the National Portrait Gallery, London. The cross at Charing Cross is also his design.

Reading the lectures he delivered on architecture at the Royal Academy in 1874 I came across this prophetic passage:

> I much fear we may drift into anarchy from the present rage for lofty buildings. I cannot doubt that the healthiness of London, as compared with many other cities, has been much promoted by the circumstance that its buildings have been, as a rule, of moderate height. If everyone is now to be at liberty to make his house a Tower of Babel, it is much to be feared that the evils he may cause will not be architectural only.

He seems to have foreseen traffic chaos and foresmelled petrol and diesel fumes.

***

Style on Road and Rail

27 June 1960

৪০ পেও

I t is odd that railway architecture in its beginnings was so splendid and that early buildings connected with motor transport were so flashy and ugly.

Think of such structures as the Britannia Bridge over the Menai Strait by Robert Stephenson and Francis Thompson (1845–50), Chester General Station by the same architects (1844–8), the Arch

(1835) and Great Hall (1846) at Euston by the Hardwicks, viaducts such as those at Congleton, Ledbury, Folkestone, Wolverton and Digwell, and the tunnel entrances and bridges Brunel designed for the Great Western in the 1840s.

Compare them with the brash concrete garages along our main roads and outside our towns which were built just before the last war — and even since.

You know the sort of thing. Stepped battlements or else a façade of concrete which looks like an enormous modernistic fireplace with little garden sheds behind it. A popular style for these garages was a sort of futuristic-bogus-modern with corner windows and oblong towers looking like an early film about the future from a script by H.G. Wells.

The style still persists in some of the remoter counties. But now that we have ceased to think of motor cars as horseless carriages, and have come to consider road transport as providing the main arteries of our island, a transport architecture could arise which is light, graceful and occasionally magnificent.

I am thinking particularly of certain dual carriage-way main roads such as that which curves down from Bix to the Henley Fair Mile, grandly landscaped with its flowering shrubs in the middle and its uneven coastline either side of woodland and grass shores, or the Guildford by-pass sweeping down from the Hog's Back towards Godalming.

Part of the Road

On the other hand, the lack of consideration for landscape and the architecture of the bridges down the M1 are matters of lasting regret.

Some of the more recent buildings connected with motors are impressive, as though a new, light, clean and portable style might arise as a natural and harmonious adjunct to our main roads.

Filling stations are really the equivalent of those little halts in wood and corrugated iron which used to diversify our delightful branch railways. Just as the halts were part of the railway and seemed to belong to it rather than to the local cottages and farms, so should filling stations be part of the road.

I don't think it is any good thatching them or trying to make them look like old castles. They must be simple and obvious without being strident as so many of them are now because of the rival claims to perfection in their products made by the various petrol companies.

A thing which has not improved in road transport architecture is lettering. The old railway companies knew about lettering and there is a certain attempt at uniformity and proportion in the signs on M1, but filling stations are often spoiled by needlessly hideous petrol advertisements. One sees a well-designed filling station or garage on to which advertisements have been stuck by an alien and insensitive brute.

The design of garages and service stations is no simple matter. The regulations about storing petrol, about exits and entrances and where pumps may be placed, about adequate room for cars to turn (for instance, a Rolls Phantom V is nearly 20 feet long and has a turning circle of well over 41 feet, while a Fiat New 500 is less than 10 feet long and has a turning circle 28 feet 3 inches in diameter, and both have to be catered for) are only some of the problems.

The local authority has to be satisfied and designer and owner will probably have to consult the local planning officer, the highway authority, the Ministry of Transport and Ministry of Power, and chief officer of police before the design is passed.

International Touch

In *Garages and Service Stations*, by Rolf Vahlefeld and Friedrich Jacques (Leonard Hill. £3 3s.), we have a German book which covers thoroughly the whole subject. It is more informative than inspiring.

And among the many Continental examples of private and public garages, multi-storey garages and filling stations shown in their plans and elevations there is nothing so dramatic and impressive as the London Transport Executive's bus garage at Stockwell, which was designed by Adie, Button and Partners with Mr Beer as consulting engineer (1953–4).

But this book shows that an international and inoffensive style of road architecture is coming into existence to compensate for the decline in design of British Railways.

Despair seems to have gripped the British Transport Commission so firmly that it has given up all consideration of the appearance of its heritage. A penny-wise pound-foolish policy has decided that the line from Manchester to London is to have overhead cables for its electrification. Only the Southern Railway will continue with the present ground-level system.

Blot on the Scene

The existing stanchions 30 feet high on either side of the track and 60 yards apart have been put up without any consideration of their appearance whatever. They have been clamped on to bridges and made to deface tunnel entrances in a clumsy manner worthy of the Central Electricity Board doing its worst in a village. The effect of these cables over the country may be seen already between Manchester and Crewe and in the Peak District.

Railway lines, their stations and signals, have been assimilated into our landscape as happily as our roads. But these stanchions are quite out of scale with our scenery and are soon to ruin for good hundreds of miles of it.

We have never been told what are the comparative costs and efficiency of ground-level electrification, diesel traction and this overhead system. Even if the last is cheaper, surely its extra cost is nothing compared with the incalculable harm these stanchions will do to what is left of British scenery. We are always having to sacrifice landscape to money, and soon nothing but money will be left.

The British Transport Commission is a law unto itself and need consult no one about the harm it does. It follows out its mandate to the letter.

***

Back to Bed and Breakfast

25 July 1960

☙ C3

S tanding in the quiet and attractive little town of Kirkby Lonsdale in the quiet and magnificent little county of Westmorland, I gazed across the Market Square to the Royal Hotel. Before Queen Adelaide waved to the crowds from its first-floor window it had been called something else. From then on it was Royal.

Seeing this well-proportioned small building, late Georgian in style and of local grey stone with a blue slate roof, like the rest of the town, I thought about the neglected and interesting subject of British hotel architecture.

It is remarkable how old hotels in country towns succeed in looking like what they are – something more public than the town house of a local landlord, less official than the Town Hall, yet obviously once (if not always now) the social centre of the town where the farmers had their ordinaries and where local notables danced in a grand room.

The Bear Hotel, Devizes; the Raven, Shrewsbury; the Rutland Arms, Bakewell; the White Hart, Salisbury; the Stamford Hotel, Stamford, Lincs, are a few of the many hundred handsome Georgian hotels which survive in all the old towns of the United Kingdom and Ireland.

Room at the Inn

It was not until the late eighteenth century that the chief inns of England were renamed hotels. Until then a house which gave you a room of your own where you were your own master was always called an inn. It was the successor of the hospitality of the monasteries.

Now the word 'inn' is associated with what used to be called an ale house, where you go for a drink but not for accommodation. In Georgian days people stayed at an inn only when they were forced to do so by the length of their journey. English literature was more full of complaints about their discomforts than praise of their merits until Dickens made them romantic.

The first hotels built with the title of hotel from the start were in watering places. One of the first must be the Clifton Hotel and Assembly Rooms, whose handsome front still looks down Clifton Mall. The Queen's Hotel, Cheltenham (1837), still dominates the end of that leafy stucco Promenade. The seaside resorts then springing up, in crescent and terrace, along the shingly shores had their hotels. Mostly these places were for invalids taking water cures at the wells or by the sea.

With the Trains

The next great group of hotels came with the railways. In intention they may have been no more than an extension of the Georgian posting inn, a place where you stopped for a night on your journey. They were also an advertisement for the railway age, with stock rooms, coffee rooms and banqueting halls for the new commercial classes.

The North Midland by Frances Thompson and the Royal by Richard Wallace, both at Derby, about 1840, the Paragon, Hull, by G.T. Andrews (1847–8), the Station Hotel, York, by the same architect, and the North Staffordshire at Stoke-on-Trent by R.A. Stent (1850) were among the first.

London followed suit with its hotels at termini: the Great Western by P.C. Hardwick (1850–53), Great Northern by Lewis Cubitt (1850), Charing Cross and Cannon Street by E.M. Barry (1860), the Grosvenor, Victoria, by J.T. Knowles (1860) and St Pancras by Sir Gilbert Scott (1867).

These buildings were something the like of which had never been seen before, each bigger than the largest country houses of the past, with the principal rooms on the ground floor and many more bedroom floors above them than are seen on any private dwelling. They therefore taxed the sense of proportion of their designers, who had to make something which looked imposing but not top heavy. When we look at these vast piles we must admit that their architects succeeded. They are clearly hotels and now an accepted part of the landscape.

Inside they had to be temptingly planned – an imposing entrance hall, a noble staircase, large reception rooms, palatial dining rooms to make businessmen feel ducal.

Where the railways led, the resorts followed: the Hydros at Ilkley and Matlock, the Grand at Scarborough by C. Brodrick (1863–7), the Palace, Southend-on-Sea, and the many turreted and terracotta wonders in every watering place.

'No expense spared' was the watchword of those spacious Victorian days. These hotels were the palaces of the new middle class.

The last crop of great hotels was mainly for the Americans, done in exotic style so as to suggest both New York and Paris. This phase brought the finest hotel as architecture in Britain – the Ritz, designed by Mewes and Davis of London and Paris, in 1905. It was the first steel-framed building to be put up in London. Its Louis Seize style is most beautifully detailed, down to the chairs and tables and cutlery.

Next to the Ritz in splendour and considered detail were the Adelphi, Liverpool, by R.F. Atkinson (1912), the Waldorf, London, by A. Marshall Mackenzie with an interior by A.J. Davis of the Ritz, and the Piccadilly Hotel (1906), London, designed by that great architect Norman Shaw in his old age.

Hotels today are built on different principles. The idea is to get in as many bedrooms as possible by means of built-in furniture and low ceilings. The reception rooms are not so lofty. The restaurants are less imposing.

In New York all the old Edwardian hotels have been altered on their ground floors so as to get in another storey of bedrooms. The splendour has gone.

The Royal Hotel in Bloomsbury, and the new Westbury in Bond Street, are symptomatic of this change in London. They are built with money-making in mind more than for the gleeful ostentation of Victorian and Edwardian days. Nor do they perform the social functions of Georgian country town hotels.

We are back to bed and breakfast at an inn.

***

Bridges Elegant or Ugly

19 September 1960

ଌଓ

It is difficult to make a bridge look ugly, though this rare feat has been achieved in the viaducts over MI. It was achieved in the last century by the cast-iron railway bridge over the Thames at Charing Cross, London, but I do not think the beauty of a bridge is dependent on its material. The eighteenth-century cast-iron bridges of Shropshire – including that at Ironbridge itself – are all handsome to look at, and there are forty-two of them in the county.

Concrete, such as is used for the lumpy and awkward looking things which cross MI, has also produced some of the finest bridges in the world. An early and little appreciated example of a concrete bridge is that by Maxwell Ayrton over the Thames at Twickenham (c. 1930). On the whole, foreign civil engineers, and in particular the Italians, who seem to have inherited the Roman genius for bridge building, are far ahead of this country in exciting and handsome designs in reinforced concrete.

The construction of motorways in Britain, as well as saving old towns and villages from disproportionate heavy traffic, will, if they are built with an eye to changes in local scenery and contour, be an addition to the landscape. Here concrete, instead of wasting itself in ugly lamp standards and needless kerbstones, can be given its opportunity for bridges and viaducts. British engineers will benefit from experiments made on the Continent.

Religious Links

We are all today aware of the beauty of bridges because we live in a time when structure is more appreciated aesthetically than decoration. Yet I doubt if the builders of the earliest bridges considered them beautiful at all. Primitive man associated river crossings with evil spirits. You will remember Jacob at the ford.

Even in Britain the Devil gave his name to bridges, and bridge builders had to have their activities sanctified by religion. One of the titles of the Pope is Pontifex Maximus – the Supreme Bridge-builder.

In England bridges were long under the care of monasteries and later of religious guilds. Wedged between the houses that were built over the sluices of Old London Bridge was the chapel of St Thomas of Canterbury. There are still chapels on the mediaeval bridges at Rotherham and Wakefield in Yorkshire, St Ives in Hunts, and Bradford-on-Avon, Wilts.

Whether they had chapels on them or not, the old bridges of England were usually built on wooden piles, and sometimes on sacks of wool, on which the stone piers were erected. These piers had to be thick enough to stand the thrust of the arches of the bridge. The parapet of the bridge generally went out in a V shape over the cutwater of each pier.

Superb examples of long mediaeval stone bridges remain at Bideford, Devon; over the Trent at Swarkestone, Derby; the Elvet Bridge at Durham; and at Ludlow, Shropshire.

The men who built them were not consciously architects, as must have been the builders of abbeys and churches, but local men who constructed in a traditional manner. They had their equivalents in the builders of the great tithe and threshing barns where roof construction in the mediaeval manner went on until the last century.

In Cornwall for instance, where there was naturally a time lag when the Duchy was more cut off from England than it is today, there is a bridge over the Amble at Trewornan which people think is as old as the splendid mediaeval stone-arched bridge over the Camel at Wadebridge nearby. But Trewornan Bridge, though it has pointed arches and cutwaters like Wadebridge, was built in the eighteenth century.

It is not an early example of Gothic revival, but a late example of the Gothic tradition of construction surviving into Georgian times. Many of those stone bridges in the cwms of Wales and the combes of Devon may well be no older than Georgian.

First Awakening

I think people first became aware of bridges as ornamental objects in the eighteenth century. Architects going on the Grand Tour must have seen the Pons Aemilius in Rome (179 BC), the bridge at Rimini (AD 20), or the magnificent bridge of six arches which the Romans built at Alcantara, Spain, in AD 109.

What is more natural than that an English nobleman should want a round-arched bridge, decorated with classical motives, over the river or the lake in his park? Hence James Paine's elegant three-arched bridge over the Derwent at Chatsworth (1761–2), Roger Morris's Palladian bridge at Wilton (1736–7), and Vanbrugh's vast bridge over the little Cotswold river Glyme at Blenheim (1705–20).

The local highway authorities, now that the roads were being more used, employed architects to make elegant structures where before there had been deep fords or what were then considered crude Gothic structures with pointed arches.

Architects generally designed bridges as a sideline, though there were some who specialised in bridges, as for instance John Gwynne who built the English Bridge, Shrewsbury (1768–74), Atcham Bridge, Shropshire (1769–71), Worcester Bridge (1771–80), Magdalen Bridge, Oxford (1772–82), and Robert Mylne, who built the Old Bridge, Glasgow (1774), Old Blackfriars Bridge, London (1760–69), and several more since demolished.

Civil engineering was not a separate profession from architecture until early in the last century. But the coming of cast iron, and with it the canals, meant that a man like Thomas Telford (1757–1834), soon gave up the architecture in which he had been trained as a young man and went in entirely for bridge and canal and road construction.

Telford was among the first to use the suspension form of bridge in this country, hanging the road from chains supported by the bridge piers. His greatest suspension bridge is that over the Menai Strait (1826), but I think Brunel's suspension bridge over the Avon Gorge at Clifton, designed when he was only twenty-four, though not built until much later, is more elegant.

Engineer and Architect

For the past century and a half bridges have been regarded almost solely as the job of civil engineers. The railways gave these engineers their greatest scope and some of the finest bridges in the world were the result – the Maidenhead Bridge for the Great Western Railway by I.K. Brunel, with its flat arches of brick – more daring than and as elegant as the contrasting eighteenth-century road bridge nearby.

Then there is Saltash Bridge, also by Brunel (1860), and the great Forth Bridge by Sir James Fowler (1890). Robert Stephenson designed the Royal Border Bridge at Berwick, the Britannia

Tubular Bridge close to Telford's suspension bridge over the Menai, and the High Level Bridge at Newcastle upon Tyne.

Civil engineers have given the world the bridges of New York, Niagara, Sydney Harbour, San Francisco. Whether their construction has been cantilever, suspension or girder they have made a new revelation of the possibilities of steel and concrete.

It is envy of this that has made so many architects today wish themselves civil engineers, with what unfortunate results. Conversely, some civil engineers seem to have forgotten the architectural qualities which civil engineering deserves.

This does not mean that an architect must be called in to add the decoration, as happened when Sir Reginald Blomfield applied his ornament to the new bridge at Lambeth. But it certainly does mean that aesthetic advice should have been sought before the viaducts over M1 were built.

***

Commerce and Ostentation

12 December 1960

૭૦ ભ

Most of us belong to the generation which think that decorations are immoral. Simplicity has been lording it almost since good King Edward died.

The decoration of buildings with anything permanent, like stone mouldings and cornices, was thought wrong for the following reasons: it was insincere because it disguised the construction; it showed that the architect was frightened of bare space and could not use proportion as decoration in itself; decoration collected dust; it was a reproduction of the details of the past and therefore not a true expression of the modern age.

'Clean, modern lines' were all the vogue until we found that we needed something more. So today the modern architect of large blocks of offices and flats made of prefabricated materials lets himself go with decoration. He does not call it such. He calls it 'cladding' and he clothes the walls of his steel structures with hanging slabs of glass in primary colours, or mosaics of coloured crazy paving. Then he has a sumptuous entrance (not in the middle as that would be too traditional) and if there is a blank external wall he scribbles in some heraldry or vague sculptures in low relief.

Men of Genius

There is no doubt that it takes a man of genius to use the age-old mouldings of the Gothic and classical periods on a building when materials, construction and proportion are not dependent on them. To me the Woolworth Building in New York (by Cass Gilbert, 1913), the first really tall skyscraper in that city, is still the most successful in outline. This is because the architect used Gothic mouldings and decoration of enormous size, and, I suspect, of enormous cost, but in scale with the building.

The Liver Building in Liverpool (by Walter A. Thomas, 1908) is another commercial example.

On the whole, however, attempts to clothe steel-constructed buildings with brick or stone to make them look like blown-up imitations of Wren's part of Hampton Court are rarely successful.

Yet we want decorations and gaiety in our streets. At Christmas, at exhibitions and at local fairs we are permitted them in temporary form. The grey chasm of Regent Street, in London, is hung with angels blowing trumpets. Traders' associations arrange communal decorations in street and market square.

Commerce justifiably demands ostentation. Its styles of decoration change with the times, which is why shop fascias are only skin-deep. For instance, the black glass and stainless steel which were the rage in the thirties are being changed today to wood and mosaic.

There are certain trades whose styles of presenting their wares have not changed, and which have benefited our public streets by remaining distinctive. France has better examples of these than our own country. I have often thought what an attractive book of coloured photographs could be made of French patisseries and of the way in which Parisian butchers display their meat.

The first shops were booths. From always being set up in the same place these booths became permanent. Monastic records from the twelfth century onwards are full of complaints about shops and sheds set up against abbey buildings without leave.

The earliest shops of a permanent sort consisted of one apartment, with a narrow door and a broad window without glass. This was closed at night by a wooden shutter, hinged at top and bottom and divided in the middle so that the upper half served as an awning and the lower half as a table. Today there are still some tradesmen who display their goods in shops open to the street, particularly fishmongers and greengrocers.

Shop windows divided across the middle and opened in their lower halves in suitable weather are survivals of the mediaeval booth.

A Splendid Row

The extensive use of glass, which came in from the eighteenth century onwards, changed the design if not the character of most shops. The open-booth type of shop was not suitable for highly finished valuable wares. The trader liked to live above his shop, and thus it came about that house and shop were conceived as a single design.

A splendid late Georgian row of shops in Woburn Walk, behind St Pancras Church, London, has recently been sympathetically restored by the Borough Council.

The largest extents of Georgian shops survive in arcades, a way of shopping that is again becoming increasingly popular now that main streets are full of vehicles and petrol fumes. The finest of these are the Royal Arcade at Newcastle upon Tyne, which has been threatened with destruction, and the Corridor at Bath. Of all the arcades in London the most attractive architecturally is the Piccadilly Arcade, which is Edwardian.

Throughout the British Isles the only trade which has maintained a distinctive position since the eighteenth century for the display of its goods is that of the pharmaceutical chemist. Most old towns have at least one who has preserved his shop front and who maintains inside his shop those large glass bottles with coloured liquids, mahogany shelves holding jars of various colours and with gold tops, weighing scales with a plush seat and row upon row of drawers whose contents are indicated in Latin abbreviations on china labels. I think particularly of one in Clifton Mall with all these fittings and a painted ceiling.

Silversmiths and watchmakers maintain a long tradition of black paint on the outside of the shop the better to show up the silver there, and dark velvet on the display shelves of gold and jewels.

Confectioners favour white outside and within. Tobacconists often still sell walking sticks and have the statue of a Highlander standing near the shop door, while at the back you may see some Turkish-style woodwork which once opened into a cigar divan.

The haberdashery trade still keeps up a display of lace and underwear and ties hung over brass rods suspended from the ceiling – a fluttering landscape through which once dashed those wooden balls containing change, along tram lines, from the counting house to the counters.

Few Barbers' Poles

The barber's striped pole has almost disappeared and so has the huge gold boot hung over the shoe shop, though I know of a fine one in Maidstone.

The ornate gas lanterns with coloured glass which used to descend from gin palaces and beer shops have been removed in favour of 'clean, modern lines' of neon strip lighting. Sometimes you may find a florist's shop which is still a conservatory, though the market garden on which it stood has long since been built over. Sometimes, too, you will find an oil and colour man with his red, wooden jar above the outside of the shop, and brushes, hardware and packets of birdseed pressed against the crowded windows.

Individual methods of display peculiar to certain trades diversify our public streets. It will be a great pity if they disappear in the uniformity of supermarkets and new shopping centres.

***

How the Planners Met Their Bannockburn

13 February 1961

೮⊃ Ꮷ

I attended an historic public meeting last month in the attractive Scottish town of Kelso. Its significance can hardly be overemphasised.

In England, where we are often bewildered by county and municipal secrecy about 'development' plans, where we never know, until too late, what 'they' – the all-powerful officials of government and their local authorities and councillors – are going to do where we live, where Messrs Cotton and Clore or their lesser equivalents may at any moment strike at some loved landmark, and replace it with a rent-collecting slab, the example of Kelso will be encouraging not only to Scotland but to the rest of the United Kingdom.

Kelso is a Border town on the banks of the Tweed, the shallow roar of whose waters, leaping with salmon, may be heard from its prospect terraces. It has over 4,000 inhabitants. It is the centre of a seven-pointed star and serves as the market town of a surrounding farming district largely composed of great estates owned by peers, baronets and un-enobled lairds who take a great part in local affairs, so that, more than most places, it has the air of a settled agricultural economy.

Splendid Approaches

It is not on any main road, the chief routes to Scotland passing some miles off to the east and west of it. From all approaches the leafy town skyline, punctuated by spires and turrets, is dominated by the great, square Romanesque tower of the ruined thirteenth-century Abbey at one end. At the other is the graceful and highly original spire of St John's Kirk (1885) by Pilkington, a wildly daring architect.

The Scots, who have provided the majority of the great architects of the United Kingdom (Gibbs, Chambers, the Adam brothers, Telford, Rennie, Pilkington, Norman Shaw, Mackintosh and Comper, to name a few who have left their mark on England) are either severe and four-square in their buildings or more madly extravagant with strange shapes and carvings than any other architects.

Of all the approaches to Kelso the most splendid is that from the south after the road leaves Northumberland between Wark and Sprouston and enters a land of wooded parks and 'policy dykes' (in English, park walls).

Two great stretches of parkland merge to provide Kelso's foreground. In the distance is Floors Castle, a towered and regular composition in golden local stone largely attributed to the late Georgian architect Playfair, on a grassy slope above Tweed, and preserving a further stretch of parkland on the opposite bank between Tweed and Teviot.

In the foreground is Springwood Park with the elegant Greek entrance gate (by Gillespie Graham, 1825) to the now demolished house. Spanning Tweed is John Rennie's stone five-arched bridge (1799–1803), with coupled columns between the arches in the manner of his old Waterloo Bridge in London.

Thus Greek simplicity and landscape gardening in the sweeping picturesque manner of the late eighteenth century form a setting for the romantic outline of abbey and town. The bridge leads by pleasant Georgian houses – of which Ednam House with its plaster ceilings and Gothic pavilion is the best – to one of the finest market squares I have seen. It is wide, cobbled and surrounded by three and four-storey houses, mostly Georgian. There is a charming classic Town Hall.

Cobbled streets and alleys lead into the square which retains a sense of enclosure and dignity. Except for one ill-adjusted bank and some very ugly concrete lamp standards of old-fashioned pattern Kelso square and indeed the setting of the town are as near perfect as they can be.

Roxburghshire County Council proposed to widen the roads into the square by destroying some of the houses, to widen the roadway of the bridge and to remove the elegant Greek gates from the southern approach to it. There were even fears, unfounded, that the town was to be turned into a through route for some kind of heavy traffic.

Views Sought

The county's plans for cutting about the town were exhibited in the Town Hall and the Provost and the Town Council encouraged the people to express their views at ward meetings. The result was that before the plans became hard set, a Kelso Preservation Society was formed with Mr F. Douglas-Whyte, a member of both Town and County Council, as chairman. An inaugural meeting of the Society, with the Duke of Roxburghe, Lord Molson and the Provost on the platform, was held in a public hall thronged with people of Kelso and the neighbourhood.

Local opinion expressed itself clearly and without rancour. County councillors moved from defensive to the cooperative. The Minister of the Parish Kirk objected to the proposed destruction of his manse. Others protested against the proposed removal of the handsome Springwood gates beyond the far end of the bridge.

It looks as though the square will not now be opened so that its sense of enclosure and its proportions are spoiled. There was no doubt of the feeling of the meeting against these and other proposals. The meeting was not obstructive nor was it heated. It was intent and practical and essentially non-political.

Good Example

I could not help thinking, when I came away from it, that here, as Hugh Molson said in his speech, was an example of democracy working on town planning. There was cooperation with the people who were to be 'planned' and consideration for their objections.

One would like such a thing to be possible in England, unvitiated by party politics, secrecy and those private understandings with speculative builders which we suspect.

The Kelso meeting came about largely because there is a remarkable outside voluntary body to sponsor it and to obtain speakers. This is the National Trust for Scotland, which performs the functions not only of the English National Trust, but also those equivalent to the Council for the Preservation of Rural England, the Society for the Protection of Ancient Buildings, the Georgian Group, the Victorian Society, the Civic Trust and all the other amenity societies necessary for a crowded country.

Perhaps because Scotland is considerably smaller and less heavily populated, except in such cities as Glasgow, such a meeting as that at Kelso is easier to organise. Even so, this is not a reason why such meetings should not be started in England with cooperation between local authorities, Ministries and the rapidly increasing amenity societies.

In such a way true expressions of local feeling and opinion can be expressed and noted without the expense of a public inquiry to which valuable witnesses are often afraid to come because they are too busy or too timid to face the lengthy browbeating process of the law.

***

A City Dying at the Heart

10 April 1961

&

Birmingham is left to get on with its own prosperity. Some call it the stomach of the world: raw materials, particularly metals, are brought to it to be digested.

Few outside it appreciate the strong character of this now elderly offspring of the Industrial Revolution. Few cities have more to show and do less about preserving a remarkable inheritance of architecture.

See Birmingham in the late eighteenth century when there were only 30,000 inhabitants and not the million and more there are now. It must have looked, on its three hills above the Rea and Tame confluence, rather as does the little Northamptonshire town of Irthlingborough seen from that romantic railway from Peterborough (East) to Northampton – pale pink brick houses and a skyline pricked by spires and a few chimneys.

It was a place of wide squares and terraces and crescents and Renaissance churches. The most notable – St Philip's (1711, Thomas Archer), now the cathedral, and St Paul's (1779, R. Ekyns) – survive.

On a heath outside the town stood Soho Hall, newly erected (1762) for Matthew Boulton by Samuel Wyatt. Here Boulton and his partner James Watt used steam-driven machinery and produced superb silver-plated designs for candlesticks and trays.

An upright chest made of folding doors studded with Matthew Boulton's original moulds survives to this day in a factory in the jewellery quarter of the city. In Birmingham the word 'jeweller' has a wider meaning than just ornaments and rings.

The Soho factory of Boulton and Watt was made to look like a country house with a lawn in front and the factory chimney shrouded in a wood. The Hall survives with its Sheraton furniture. This Georgian tradition of making a factory look like a country house survived in Eikington's factory in Newhall Street when electro-plate was invented to bring the death of the Sheffield plating carried on in Birmingham.

In Regency and early Victorian times the town spread into the country, notably to Edgbaston, the pleasantest, leafiest suburb in the heart of any industrial city that I know: stucco villas, valleys and broad winding roads.

Here lived the more prosperous merchants and professional classes. The smaller tradesmen built workshops in their back gardens in the centre of the city and lived over their shops. One of these, a picture frame carver, was the father of Burne-Jones. Where he lived in Bennett's Hill, which is crossed by Waterloo Street, is the only considerable survival in the centre of Birmingham of its splendid Regency street architecture.

Cobbled streets of old brick two-storey houses with handsome cast-iron lettering at the corners are disappearing from such inner suburbs as Hockley-in-the-Hole, Soho and Winson Green. They were the birthplace of that industry of brass buttons, collar studs, guns, bicycles, motor cars glassware, wire and pens and nibs and papier mâché which made Birmingham famous.

The rambling black workshops of the old jewellery quarter, where pale, spectacled craftsmen work with blowlamps in surroundings which look like an old eighteenth-century print, are being deserted for new hygienic factories on the new estates — driven out by the planners 'for their own good'.

In 1837 the London to Birmingham railway arrived in Birmingham, stopping at Philip Hardwick's Ionic portico of Curzon Street Station, Birmingham's answer to his 'Great Arch' at Euston. Classical temples adorned the city in the form of churches, chapels, market and public buildings. The old Town Hall (1834–50, by Joseph Hansom) is a reproduction of the temple of Jupiter Stator in Rome.

But there was a reaction against too many temples, and a good case could be made out for the birth of the more serious side of the Gothic Revival in Birmingham.

Thomas Rickman (1776–1841), the Quaker architect who invented the terms 'Norman', 'EE' [Early English], 'Decorated' and 'Perpendicular', built several churches here, where he died. Sir Charles Barry in 1832 designed the King Edward VI School, since demolished, in a style that was a foretaste of his Houses of Parliament.

Pugin designed the soaring, impressive and thin Roman Catholic cathedral of St Chad (1839) and its Bishop's House, and he decorated Oscott College. Hardman carried out Pugin's designs in stained glass and metal in his Birmingham studio. Burne-Jones brought his Pre-Raphaelite friends to the town, and the City Art Gallery has the most notable collection of their works.

J.L. Pearson built two of his finest churches here, St Alban (1879–81) and St Patrick. One of the most original and refined of the architects of the Gothic Revival was a Birmingham man – W.H. Bidlake, whose masterpiece, St Agatha's, Sparkbrook (1889–91), and other churches in his individual style, adorn the city.

Like sounding brass is the era of Joseph Chamberlain, and symbolised by the rich Victorian baroque of Yeoville Thomason's Council House (1879), begun in his mayoralty. French chateaux and Germanic castles rise in terracotta and stone for official use.

Prosperity's Echoes

Birmingham became a city in 1889. The Grosvenor Banqueting Room of the Grand Hotel still seems to echo with official speeches lauding commercial prosperity.

Sir Aston Webb and Ingress Bell, not content with the fantastic Law Courts (1887–91), designed the vast University (1906–9) with its campanile tower and its crescent plan and great hall – the largest in the Midlands. It must be the origin of the phrase 'redbrick university'.

The other side of Birmingham is radical, Morris-y, and 'work of each for weal of all'. Horrified by Birmingham's slums, which had also shocked Pugin and his local followers, the Quaker firm of Cadbury built Bournville in 1895.

It was second only to Port Sunlight in age as a pioneer industrial garden suburb. It still stands, a place of grassy ways, churches and halls, but never a public house.

'And Birmingham shall be a famous City, of white stone, full of brave architecture, carved and painted,' wrote Burne-Jones in 1885. 'Politics quite needless since the fight has been won … advertisements penal and the newspapers, if needed at all, in strict rhyme and metre.'

The motor car has strangled Birmingham, congesting its centre despite an ingenious one-way traffic system and spreading out the villas of the rich to what once were country places – Solihull, Sutton Coldfield, Henley-in-Arden and even Stratford-upon-Avon.

These newer detached houses are often shapely, well planned and of materials which harmonise with Birmingham's home counties. But as Birmingham spreads over the Midlands its planners are so cutting about the heart of the city that soon the old individualistic Birmingham will be dead.

***

The Most Beautiful City in England

8 May 1961

෨෬

Three hundred years ago Bristol was the second largest city in Britain. The fact that it is now only sixth in order of size does not diminish its great interest, for Bristol has escaped the worst phases of nineteenth- and twentieth-century industrialism.

Though it was cruelly bombed in the last war, and the little churches and narrow lanes with their tall overhanging houses in the centre of the city largely destroyed, Bristol is still for me the most beautiful, interesting and distinguished city in England.

Anyone wanting to know how English towns grew, and to see the best examples of every phase of architecture, excluding the present, can find the whole history of England in the stone and brick of Bristol. Bristol has everything and makes no show of it. So far as I know it is little visited by tourists, but it is far more worth visiting than some of the recognised 'beauty spots'.

The long, low and too little known cathedral contains some of the most surprising and exciting Gothic architecture in Europe. In about 1320 a designer of genius constructed a great stone-vaulted chancel lit not by a clerestory, but from the narrow aisles, whose ribbed stone roofs are ingeniously constructed so as to allow the uninterrupted passage of light from the aisle windows into the choir.

Perfect Proportions

That vigorous and bold Victorian architect G.E. Street continued the fourteenth-century scheme of vaulting and lighting when he completed the nave in 1868.

Another of Bristol's pre-Reformation buildings is the church of St Mary Redcliffe, described by Queen Elizabeth I as 'the fairest, goodliest and most famous parish church in England'. With its fan-vaulted nave, choir and narrow transepts it is indeed like a cathedral inside, and, unlike most cathedrals, it is largely all of a piece, except for the rich and earlier north porch. It has a perfection of lofty proportions which challenges comparison with two other great buildings of the Perpendicular period – St George's, Windsor, and King's College Chapel, Cambridge.

The heart of Bristol continued to look mediaeval until forty years ago, when ships thrust their bowsprits almost into the windows of the tram cars and their rigging stood out against the sky in a setting of lace-like Somerset church towers.

I recall a ghost story about someone putting up for the night in a seventeenth-century Bristol house down by the waterside, and waking at two in the morning to hear the rumbling of barrels and loud Elizabethan oaths, and looking out to see a ship being manned and loaded to fight the Spanish Armada.

Bristol throve on the wine trade, the spice trade with the East Indies and the slave trade. The atmosphere of these days still survives in King Street, notably in the gabled half-timbered house called Llandoger Trow (1669). In King Street, too, is the eighteenth-century Theatre Royal, inside very much as it was when first built in 1764, and still in use.

As the city prospered its merchants left the narrow lanes to live in squares, of which the largest, Queen Square, named after Queen Anne in whose reign it was built, is now spoiled by a main road crossing it diagonally.

The differences between the eighteenth-century houses of Bristol and those of Bath are two: Bristol houses are often of brick with stone dressings, whereas Bath houses are all of stone with more impressive fronts; the Bath houses were built mostly as lodgings for the season, while the Bristol merchants' houses were built as permanent residences and money was lavished on their interiors. Many a fine ceiling in plasterwork, much panelling and many marble chimney pieces survive in houses which are comparatively plain outside.

There was a Bristol school of plasterwork, a sort of West Country baroque, and in a house called the Royal Fort, in the precincts of the University, there is a staircase hall with a plaster pattern of trailing vines and animals.

Perhaps as a compensation for the slave trade, Bristol developed a Nonconformist conscience and is still associated with the

Evangelical school of thought. Wesley's New Room in Horsefair (1739) was most sensitively restored by Sir George Oatley. This and the Unitarian Chapel in Lewin's Mead (1787) and the Friends' Meeting House (1747) are unspoiled examples of Puritan worship, the first two with their high pulpits, galleries and pews.

Largest in England

Bristol's biggest surprise is Clifton – a sort of Bath consisting of Regency crescents and terraces looking over the Avon Gorge to the blue hills of Somerset. The finest of them in size is Royal York Crescent – the largest crescent in England – and there are many handsome late Georgian terraces of which the grandest are The Mall, with its Assembly Rooms, and Vyvyan Terrace.

Steep hills lead to steps: steps lead to terraces: and everywhere there are glimpses of gardens, delicate verandahs, lawns and trees.

No English city has so large and leafy a Georgian suburb as Clifton. As the merchants climbed up the hill out of trade into the professions they moved to Clifton, and from their Georgian houses went out to found the Empire, starting with the John Company and culminating in the Indian Army and the ICS.

They sent the animals they found abroad to the charming Clifton Zoo, and when they came home and begat children they sent them to Clifton College, among whose pupils were Sir Henry Newbolt and the first Earl Haig.

Brunel's Fine Bridge

Of all the fine sights Clifton has to show the finest is Brunel's Suspension Bridge (1836–61), lightly hung from vast Egyptian pylae above the most spectacular part of the Avon Gorge. The setting is embosomed in woods which give glimpses of white limestone and the brown tidal waters of the Avon far below, all to be seen from a camera obscura on the hilltop.

Yet Bristol must always be honoured too for promoting the Great Western Railway from Temple Meads to Paddington and for employing Brunel as its engineer. His original station (1839–40) survives with its wooden hammer-beam roof at an obscure end of the existing building.

There are many original Victorian and Edwardian buildings in Bristol. A beautiful branch of the Bank of England by C.R. Cockerell (1844–7) in Broad Street is in the best scholarly Graeco-Roman style of the time. The Edwardian era is represented by Charles Holden's Municipal Library (1906) near the cathedral, in a modern style, very dashing and simple for its date.

In front of the Victoria Rooms (1839–41) is an exquisite Viennese baroque fountain designed by Edwin Rickards. As you climb Park Street out of old Bristol to the airy heights of Clifton you see Sir George Oatley's splendid University Tower in a Perpendicular style all of his own (1925), skilfully set so that two sides of it are visible from the main thoroughfare.

The latest prominent addition to the city is the huge monumental Classic Council House on College Green by E. Vincent Harris (1938) with gilt unicorns on its roof. Its pale brick and strong Classic stone plinth contrast with the neighbouring cathedral but do not clash.

Hidden Glories

I said at the beginning that Bristol has everything but makes no show of it. Yet its glories are hidden.

No one would know from the outside how remarkable was the inside of the cathedral. The Theatre Royal is hidden behind a poor new front. Sumptuous merchants' houses are plain outside. Clifton is invisible from the main roads of the city.

Bristol, with its steep hills and sudden squares, must be explored to be discovered. Lately it has not made the best of its superb hilly skyline. It has filled up the basin at the City Centre and planted a silly municipal garden. It has bisected Queen Square and allowed the Bath House at Arno's Castle, which contained the finest plasterwork in England, to fall into ruin. But it still remains our grandest old city, and has kept more of its individuality and variety than London itself.

***

Architecture of Death

20 November 1961

ॐ ᘓ

November is the month for remembering the departed. This is why I write about the now unpopular subject of churchyards and cemeteries and their architecture.

For the first seven centuries of Christianity, burials were occasions of joy and people attending them wore white, because faith was firm. And so it often is still with the faithful. I knew an Anglican nun who, when she was dying, told me it was a happy experience 'like packing up one's books for the end of term'.

By the Middle Ages, when Christianity became more nominal and the fear of Hell and last-minute repentance were stressed, the colour changed to black for burials.

All the same, until the Renaissance people did not usually build monuments to their own glory but churches or chapels, where prayers could be said for their own souls and those of their family. This is why you will seldom find in the churchyards of old churches named tombstones dated earlier than the seventeenth century.

But when, for reasons which it would be out of place to go into here, modern Protestantism objected to prayers for the dead, and chantry priests were no longer paid to pray for the souls of the departed, people liked to be remembered on earth in something as permanent as stone and with their name carved on it.

Great Variety

The richer landowners had splendid tombs built inside the church and this tradition went on until the last century, so that our country churches are often impressive galleries of Renaissance sculpture. The less rich were commemorated with headstones outside in the churchyard — yeoman farmers and tradesmen.

People who wonder what happened to the craftsmanship which carved the capitals and tracery of mediaeval churches can find the tradition of stone-carving carried on in the churchyard.

Look at the many different shapes for the tops of headstones which are devised even in one churchyard. Then see the splendour of the deep-cut lettering, carved out with all the spaciousness of the title page of an elegant and expensive Georgian folio book. The letters are cut deep to catch the shadows cast by the sun, particularly at midday.

Often there are charming and touching rhyming epitaphs composed by some poetical parson or village schoolmaster. Most impressive of all on the headstones of the eighteenth century are the carvings of cherubs, skulls and crossbones, ploughs, flowers, clouds and suns and sheaves of corn forming a sort of frame or headpiece to the inscription.

Alien Stone

At Olney in north Buckinghamshire there was a Georgian monumental mason of real genius. And many people must know the elaborately lovely table tombs and headstones in Burford and its neighbouring Cotswold churchyards.

Then, there are the slate tombs of Cornwall, Westmorland and Leicestershire, the Portland stone of Dorset, and in Kent and Surrey may be found attractive wooden memorials and in Shropshire there are some of iron.

It was not until late in the last century when white marble was introduced from Italy and the carving of lettering died out with the introduction of prefabricated letters mechanically inlaid into stone that churchyards began to become grim and ugly. One tomb of alien stone, be it marble or granite, in a limestone area can ruin a whole churchyard.

Until this foreign invasion, churchyards were natural places where the grass was kept down by sheep or the parson's cob. This was before the modern custom of curbs and clappings and pots of flowers.

Today parsons and parochial church councils seem to be ashamed of their churchyards looking like the natural setting the centuries have made them for the church. They try to turn them into villa gardens with crazy paving and rambler roses and birdbaths and mown grass. The old headstones are being taken up and ranged along the churchyard walls like playing cards and where the sun no longer throws up the shadows of their carving.

Thus do we strip the dignity from death and sentimentalise the inevitable.

I think this uglification and sentimentalising of country churchyards has a town origin. I think it spread from metropolitan cemeteries, which did not start ugly at all but have become white wastes of rain-streaked marble.

Here I would like to stake a plea for the retention and upkeep of those of our cemeteries which were landscaped in the grand manner of the eighteenth century and have Greek Revival entrance gates and separate Greek temples for the burial service of the Church of England and Nonconformity.

All our larger cities have them, and along their main cedar-shaded walks are ranged the imposing mausolea of once-prosperous manufacturing and professional families. The grandest of all is the Glasgow Necropolis, whose column to John Knox stands guardian over a forest of lesser Presbyterian columns and spirelets, black against the sky and looking down from the hilltop to St Mungo's Cathedral.

There is Sheffield General Cemetery (1836) with its classic chapel and gates by Samuel Worth on whose cast iron is a laurel leaf below which are the words 'Dogs not admitted' in bold late Georgian iron letters, as part of the design.

In Manchester, on the road to Hale, I saw lately another late Georgian cemetery grass-grown and forgotten, with its rusting cast-iron gates. Bristol, Liverpool and all our other larger cities have these impressive reminders of our dust.

Badly Neglected

And in London there is that strange neo-Egyptian columbarium in Highgate Old Cemetery (1839) designed by Stephen Geary. Here one can look through the grilles of the catacombs and see the rows of coffins.

In London cemeteries in particular there are often handsome tombs designed by famous architects now weed-grown and neglected. But also in these cemeteries is the dust of the great Victorians; for instance in Highgate George Eliot, Michael Faraday, Herbert Spencer, Christina Rossetti, Karl Marx, Lilly White and Mrs Henry Wood. Behind the vast Greek Revival gates of Kensal Green (1833) lie Robert Owen, Thackeray, John Leech, the Brunels, Balfe, George Cruikshank, Sydney Smith, Wilkie Collins, Anthony Trollope and that great poet Thomas Hood.

In what condition are their little visited and forgotten tombs? (We must except Karl Marx.) It would be a pity if they were to disappear under weed and rubble because no funds exist to keep their graves in order.

***

Urbs in Rure

19 February 1962

଼୨୯ ୦ଌ

I s West Suffolk to be part of London? This month it is expected that Dr Charles Hill, Minister of Housing and Local Government, will decide.

If he says yes, then four of the most beautiful towns in Britain will be changed out of recognition.

Bury St Edmunds, with its fine flint churches and abbey ruins, its Georgian houses and old theatre and Assembly Rooms, its handsome Corn Exchange and pleasant, narrow shopping streets and wide market place, has only one drawback. It is already overcrowded with traffic. The town is, all the same, a balanced community with all recognised public amenities for a population of just over 20,000. Dr Hill may add 10,000 Londoners to it.

Hadleigh is one of the most perfect small towns in England, with trees, old red brick, flint and plaster and that unassuming beauty of East Anglia which changes to glory in sunlight. It has a population of 3,000, and Dr Hill may double it.

Lavenham and Clare are large villages so famous for the beauty of their churches and old houses that they are in all the guidebooks to Britain, and much visited by tourists. To each of these villages Dr Hill may add 500 Londoners. The other towns of West Suffolk to be affected are Sudbury, Newmarket, Mildenhall, Brandon, Glemsford, Elmswell, Stanton and Haverhill.

Other Reasons

West Suffolk was the inspiration of Gainsborough and Constable. Now that Essex has been almost overrun by London, West Suffolk is the nearest unsuburbanised country to the Great Wen. If Dr Hill agrees to its suburbanisation 40,000 Londoners will be decanted into it whether they like it or not.

Although this is a tiny fraction of London's population and unlikely materially to solve the problem of London's housing, it will effectively ruin an irreplaceable asset. It will take from us in London the last surrounding deeply pastoral landscape, for in all other directions London and its influence have spread much farther.

The West Suffolk County Council welcomes these 40,000 Londoners. There is the charitable appeal of giving shelter to the homeless. There is much talk of this inundation being inevitable. There is no doubt true sincerity in these remarks for London's housing is indeed a problem. But I suspect that there are other reasons, too. The officials of local authorities naturally see an increase in their influence, possibly a rise in status, as a result of increased rates, and rescue from being absorbed by the larger and more countrified half of the county.

Then the local councillors, who consist, as do most local councils, largely of tradesmen, think that more people will bring more trade. They do not realise that the chain stores and supermarkets will put them out of business, and that light industries will drive away local industries.

They maintain that their towns and large villages are stagnant, yet all of those to which it is proposed to add Londoners are increasing in population steadily and naturally. Finally there are probably some farmers, not always the most selfless members of a country community, willing to sell land for housing and industry at a good price.

There is the other side of the picture. The local amenity societies, and the Council for the Preservation of Rural England and many private people who live in West Suffolk, have written letters of protest to their local papers. In Lavenham one of the defenders of his home town has sent a letter with 1,447 signatures to the two local MPs.

For once I feel thankful that the fate of West Suffolk, and particularly Bury St Edmunds, Hadleigh, Lavenham and Clare, is not entirely in the hands of the local authorities but Whitehall. The Minister can see that housing is a national problem. He can realise that country areas of peace and quiet, even if their tender beauty is not so obvious as to be designated a National Park, are essential to the life of the nation.

The noisier and more congested our towns become and the wider our suburbs spread, the more essential are the belts of real country, especially those, like West Suffolk, near a large city. And this is not taking into account the sacrifice of valuable agricultural land or the psychological effect of a large population of bewildered Londoners unused to country life on a settled and natural agricultural community.

Yet the housing of London and our other big cities has to be solved, and Dr Hill's choice is indeed a fearsome one, for we like to live, most of us, in a house of our own with its own bit of garden. Yet if life in England is to be endurable we will have to build more compactly, and quite often higher, in places that are already spreading too far out.

Ugly spreading places could be rebuilt more compactly, with traffic segregated from pedestrian areas. There is less harm in building upwards, if there are pleasure and peace in what is on the ground.

Indecent Word

I am also quite certain that putting Londoners into places that are already healthy and happy and balanced communities is taking away something essential and irreplaceable. Once destroyed, a glorious wool town of the Middle Ages like Lavenham, and a modest and attractive town like Hadleigh, can never be brought back to life. The sad thing is that beauty has become almost an indecent word.

There are many towns and suburbs which can take another 500 people. There is only one Lavenham, only one Clare, only one Hadleigh and only one Bury St Edmunds. Their ruination will not really solve London's housing.

The Glory that Was London

19 March 1962

The City of London is an English mystery. Behind one its gold watch beats a warm heart, but under its silk hat is a shrewd head. The head and heart are often at war, and the former usually wins, hence the modern appearance of the City, with its inhuman cliffs of rent-collecting slabs.

The mystery is ancient and wonderful, and makes the City of London different from anywhere else in England even today. Its very government is strange, and has somehow out against the LCC just as its polite and obliging police force remains independent from the Metropolitan police.

What is the Secondary and High Bailiff of Southwark doing this side of the river, and is the burden of his two duties a strain? What does the City Remembrancer remember? Does the Chief Commoner of the Court of Common Council have more power than the Lord Mayor?

These are questions to which I find it rather pleasant not to know the answer, just as in a Gothic cathedral it is satisfying to see through one arch a glimpse of more arches and screens hiding who knows what beyond.

Then there is the mystery of the eighty-two City Companies, most of which are mediaeval in origin, each with its own ceremonies and feasts when the silver is brought out and glee singers render 'Drink to me only' in the cigar smoke of after-dinner repletion. Twelve of these are the Great Companies, but no one explains why the remaining seventy are less great, even though they may have finer halls and larger liveries than the twelve great ones.

Would a man on the court of the Mercers, the chief company, consider it beneath his dignity also to be in the picturesque position of member of the court of the Gold and Silver Wyredrawers, who have no hall, poor things, and are seventy-fourth in order of precedence?

Finally, there are the City churches. Before the fire of London there were more than a hundred within the square mile of the City. Today there are only thirty-five. Eight of these are either not yet open or are awaiting restoration from bomb damage. Eight are mediaeval, twenty-one are by Sir Christopher Wren, and six are later than Wren and no less magnificent than those by the master. Indeed, the interior of St Mary Woolnoth by Nicholas Hawksmoor, and of St Botolph, Aldersgate, by an unknown late eighteenth-century architect, are two of the finest London church interiors.

The City churches almost all do splendid work today, and are much used during the week. I can remember the old pre-war days of lazy incumbents living at the seaside, coming up once a week on Sunday, and organising an occasional weekday organ recital. Those days are over, and the Church in the City is coming to life again, with daily services during the lunch hour.

I have deliberately been so unarchitectural for so long, when writing of the City, because these three elements, its government, its livery companies and its churches, distinguish this ancient place of Roman origin from the rest of London.

You can feel the change as soon as you pass eastward from Temple Bar. You notice it again as you pass out through Aldgate into the oriental mart atmosphere of Whitechapel.

Still a River Port

To the south where the Thames flops against the walls of wharves, and washes oily stone steps between the warehouses, you realise that the City is still a river port. To the north at Smithfield, with its electrically lit lanes of livers and lights and carcases, you realise the City is also a market for cattle, once driven in alive from the pastures of inland England, now carried in dead and frozen by the noisiest lorries in London.

Imagine the mediaeval City on the wide, slow-flowing Thames, held up by the sluices under London Bridge, with its houses and chapel. There it stands, white-walled in Middlesex fields, and, once in its gates, the roads are narrow and the alleys narrower still, with the timbered gables nearly touching one another overhead and the smell fearful, and the only places of quiet the numerous little churches and garths.

Crowning everything is old St Paul's with its spire, the largest cathedral in Christendom. One gets a faint flavour of this City in the churches of St Bartholomew the Great, St Helen's and St Ethelburga's. It was an East Anglian place rather like Norwich.

Now see the City rebuilt by Wren and later architects. The walls are breached and handsome red-brick houses such as still exist at Spitalfields extend into the meadows. Inside, a forest of Portland stone steeples and lead spires gathers round the mothering dome of Paul's. In the streets merchants still live over their shops and rent box pews in the parish church. The best Wren interior to survive giving an impression of those times is in St Mary at Hill, with its wealth of carved woodwork, its sword rests, high pews and marble floor all under a dome supported on four columns.

Now see the Victorian City. The merchants have moved out to big brick houses in Islington, Clapham and Streatham. Many of the churches have been demolished and their sites sold for office and warehouse blocks. Buildings are higher and dwarf the remaining Wren steeples and have even encroached on the building height round St Paul's.

There is still one place where you can see St Paul's as Wren meant you to see it, and that is on the north side, where his brick chapter house forms a warm red plinth to the upper stage of the two storeys into which he divided the exterior of his new cathedral.

The old lanes with their shops and chop and coffee houses survive for the precious lunch hours of City clerks, later to go by steam train and knife-board horse omnibus to grey-brick nearer suburbs.

Now see the City of London today. The skyline has gone. The alleys are blocked. Hardly a shopping street is left and a few churches and halls stand like museum pieces in cliffs of some of the most undistinguished copybook contemporary ever seen, even in the Middle West of America.

All That is Left

Only around Billingsgate and the doomed Coal Exchange and in a few alleys in the financial quarter and around Guildhall will you find the spirit of even the Victorian City.

Before it is all sacrificed to money and the motor car, see what is left. The old institutions are there, though the people who are 'something in the City' today mostly commute to Sussex and Surrey and have sold their grandfathers' houses in Streatham and Highbury to the 'developer'. You could park your car on the new 'Route II' in the north of the city were it permissible, for that is the only deserted street in the once glorious City of London.

***

No Place to Hide from Noise

9 July 1962

80 CB

We are becoming afraid of silence. Two or three motor cars have only to be gathered together at a recognised beauty spot for someone to turn on the wireless or take out a transistor set to drown the song of the birds and the rustle of wind in the grass.

Many people, when they enter a quiet room, automatically — even before shutting the door — rush to turn on the wireless as though quiet were as unhealthy as a cold draught.

I daresay this nervous itch for recorded music and the sound of the spoken voice is a subconscious defence we put up against the increasing industrial noise, inhuman, irregular, and often deafening to which we are daily subjected.

Noise concerns both men and buildings and it is not surprising to find it the subject of an important article in the current number of the journal of the Royal Institute of British Architects.

Anyone looking for somewhere to live in England today, however restricted his choice of district, has to consider his ears as well as his eyes. Indeed, better no view and quiet than a view and a hellish noise.

Noise from the ground is what troubles most of us and of these ground noises traffic is the most all-pervading. There is no escape for someone living, as I do, in what was once a residential cul-de-sac in the City when it becomes a route for heavy vehicles in the small hours of the morning, so that even double windows and ear plugs cannot give a night's sleep.

There is a solution. Residential streets should not be used for through traffic.

A motorcycle can make an even louder and more nerve-racking noise than a heavy lorry, and in the stillness of the night or a quiet Sunday morning, one such machine can poison a square mile of peace.

I can well understand the mentality of a young man who is crushed at home wanting to let off his inhibitions in a deafening roar on the public road. But cheaper than psychoanalysis for millions would be a law compelling manufacturers of motorcycles and two-stroke scooters to fit effective silencers to all machines.

Everybody living in an echoing street can be driven silly at night by the slamming of car doors as people park, and one invention which would considerably lessen road noise at night would be a car door which shuts without having to be slammed.

There is no legal definition of the difference between heavy and light industry, and planners often talk of 'a sprinkling of light industry' in country towns and suburbs as though it were some delicious benefit bringing prosperity, joy and peace. In no time it becomes a source of noise — lorries and workers' buses come crashing through quiet roads to the new factories and heavy plant necessitated by the expansion of the business shakes the surrounding houses and disturbs even a Sunday morning with its noise from people earning their overtime money.

Noise from the sky is an increasing menace. Throughout England airports are expanding and new ones are being built. No coordination exists for the protection of residents in the neighbourhood of an airport. This is because air travel has nothing to do with local authorities or local boundaries and is considered by those who plan it entirely in terms of air freight, regardless of those who live in the neighbourhood.

The most appalling noise from the sky is yet to come, when helicopter services are established between the airports and the cities which they serve. The Ministry of Aviation, in its recent report on the planning of helicopter stations in the London area, says:

> In cruising flight at altitudes of about 1,000 feet the noise level on the ground of the different types of helicopter should not be greater than that of traffic in a busy street at pavement level, but the noise would be heard over a wider area.

The meaning of this, the RIBA journal comments, is roughly:

> ... that the whole of Central London, including all those relatively quiet places which are sheltered from noise on the ground, but not from the air, will be subjected fairly frequently to noise levels equivalent to those on the pavements of Oxford Street; in the neighbourhood of the helicopter station they will, of course, be very much higher.

Some people thinking to escape from noise on the ground have taken refuge in tall blocks of flats high in the air. It is worth noting that tall blocks made with the latest cheap methods of construction, that is to say a tall framework whose exterior cladding is factory-made panels, are considerably less resistant to noise than even a thin brick wall.

This does not augur well for the future quiet of those who have sought refuge in height.

Finally, and more easily curable, are the noises we suffer inside a building. The worst of all are, without a doubt, in factories where heavy plant physically damages the hearing of workers who have little, if any, legal remedy, And what is monetary compensation compared with the loss of a precious faculty?

The remedy here is for the designers of plant machinery in the first place to consider noise as well as safety and efficiency. There is, I believe, no evidence that this is ever considered by designers of plant machinery and it is left to the architect of the factory to reduce the noise and at the same time to ensure an efficient plan for the working of the factory. This is usually impossible, and the best that can be effected is a very slight reduction of noise by the introduction of sound-absorbing material.

In only one respect can noise be efficiently reduced, and that is inside a house or a block of flats when it is being built. Partition walls, if enough money is spent on them, can be made soundproof. In an age which regards the spending of money on anything that will not yield a profit as slightly eccentric, I fear there is little hope of soundproofing walls except by exceptionally benevolent builders.

The sad conclusion is that noise is going to get much worse. The remedies for it seem to be so expensive and non-profit-making that we are faced with the alternatives of living underground or going to Australia, where life goes at the right pace and one can see and breathe and hear.

***

Painting the Lily of Kent

26 November 1962

₧₨

There is more variety of colour in buildings in England than many of us realise. Grey skies show up the colours more subtly than sunshine.

Apart from the famous villages and country towns along the limestone belt from Lincolnshire to Somerset, where stone varies from dark brown, through gold, to silver, there is the infinite variety of colour in counties which have very little building stone at all. I think the richest of these is Kent, the doorstep of England, the county which has been civilised since Roman times.

The colour range there is vast. The earliest buildings to survive are of blackish-blue flints roughly mortared together. They were used for castles and churches. Cut limestone was precious and had to be brought by boat up the rivers and carried by cart to provide dressings and tracery for flint churches.

The Masterpiece

Kent's greatest masterpiece, Canterbury Cathedral, is all of stone because in the Middle Ages, the age of faith, only the best and most durable material could be used for the chief cathedral of the kingdom. Anyone who has seen (as I once had the privilege of seeing) the cathedrals of Bourges, Chartres and Canterbury on three successive days can see how the last-named belongs to Christendom and the years before Europe was split up into nations.

The lesser buildings of Kent, the cottages and farms, were first of wood and plaster and quite a few of these survive. One sees them from the railway – a green mound of grass rising from flat orchard land and perched on it a square-built yeoman's farm with uneven, creamy plaster walls and overhanging upper storey in which may be seen the upright oak timbers which support the red-tiled roof.

Beside it is an oast house with weather-boarded walls, tarred black, and somewhere among the apple trees the flint walls of a church with an enormous tiled roof of orange-red like the heart of an autumn bonfire.

Saffron and Silver

From Tudor times brick was used extensively in Kent. It was made from the clay in the districts where the oaks grow. Kentish bricks at their oldest are dark red and small and were often used as dressings for flint buildings. Patterns were made of light and dark contrasting reds varied here and there with 'sanded headers', that is to say bricks glazed dark blue and pale purple and black.

In the eighteenth century, in south-east Kent, many houses had their walls hung with tiles on the weather sides and these tiles, on roofs and walls, have received a wonderful patina of saffron and silver lichens from the salt air.

Towards the end of the eighteenth century brown and yellow bricks were made, particularly in west Kent and on the sea coast. This was in the time when red brick was beginning to be thought cheap and old-fashioned. Yellow brick had a nearer approach to the look of stone. Then in Regency times the grander houses, rectories, terraces and crescents were covered with stucco and painted cream and the cheaper houses were covered with weatherboarding painted cream or covered with tar.

All these varieties of colour in Kentish building are gathered into the old streets of Canterbury and, as the brick tradition went on right through the last century, every lane, alley, and even Victorian suburban road, changes in its length in colour and texture. Browns and reds and the black and white of half-timber curve away unevenly to the termination of an old flint church, while above the chimney pots soar the magnificent silvery white towers of the cathedral.

Since the bombing of Canterbury the borough and private enterprise have, so far as domestic rebuilding in the centre of the city is concerned, kept to the scale, colour range and material of the Kentish tradition. Indeed, the new houses in the centre of old Canterbury show more consideration for the character of the city than those I have seen elsewhere in the rebuilt cities of England.

A Seemly White

One mistake has, however, been made in the recent commercial blocks, and this is the introduction of curtain-walling in glass in architect's primary colours. These smooth, sleek sheets neither mix with nor prove an agreeable contrast with a city and county whose buildings are primarily wood, brick, flint and chalk.

When there is so much colour in our buildings by reason of the materials of which they are built, you would hardly have thought it would have been necessary to add more colour in the form of paint. The only paint which looks well for the exterior woodwork of a brick, stone or stucco building is white, which is not a colour at all.

White was always used in the past, as anyone can see who looks at coloured paintings and prints of old towns and villages, for woodwork and window frames. Yet even in Canterbury, where the reds and yellows of the bricks call out for white to show them up, green and mustard-yellow and mauve are used for window frames and some superb seventeenth- and eighteenth-century houses have been permanently disfigured by a coating of mustard- or mauve- or pink-coloured cement paint, over the whole surface of what once was mellow old brick.

The rot started at the end of the last century when chocolate and green were used for painting the windows, doors and woodwork of stone and brick buildings. I think these colours were introduced because they were thought 'natural'. Chocolate was thought to look like Mother Earth and green to look like Dame Nature. Neither ever performed the services expected of them.

Since the Festival of Britain, and perhaps as a result of advertising by paint manufacturers, there has been a drive for 'gaiety'. Many a modest brick terrace, many a country cottage of plaster or local stone, has had its scale and texture destroyed by pink cement paint on the walls and green or blue paint for the woodwork.

As much damage has been done by sudden and unneighbourly eruptions of bright red and yellow paint in modest streets as has been done by new shop fascias and copybook contemporary buildings. Whole fishing ports in Cornwall which, before the war, were grey and pale-blue slate and local stone have been painted white all over, with blue paint for all woodwork.

Frantic Doors

Front doors are now primrose, pink, mauve, black and red where the traditional and seemly thing was grained wood. Ironwork, instead of being the blue-black or black it used to be painted, now takes all shades of the rainbow.

Even in a stucco Georgian terrace, where a uniform treatment of the whole front would have given the design the unity and dignity it had when it was built, each house is of a different colour.

If people will look again at the wonderful variety of natural colours there are in English buildings, some of the damage that is being done may be arrested. When the time comes for repainting the outside of the house some of its dignity may be restored, if owners will use white for wood, black for ironwork, cream for plaster, and leave the rest to nature.

***

Relics of Pomp and Circumstance

18 May 1964

֍ ☾ ☽

P ublic memorials are generally the resounding expressions of a confident age. Our own era of commercial prosperity is symbolised in the Albert Memorial (Sir Gilbert Scott, 1863–72).

There it stands glittering with mosaic, gold, bronze, polished red granite and sculptured marble, in Hyde Park on the site of the Crystal Palace, which was the first prefabricated glass and iron structure of its size in the world.

The Palace itself was packed up and re-erected on a south London height at Sydenham. But the Memorial, to its founder, the Prince Consort, is worthy of closer inspection than it gets from most people today.

The sculpture, particularly that on its eastern face by H.H. Armstead, and the figure of Prince Albert himself on his bronze throne, by J.H. Foley, is vigorous. Parts of the group entitled 'Engineering' might well be taken for something in the 1954-64 exhibition in the Tate Gallery.

There may be some justification for the view that the Albert Memorial is really a piece of goldsmith's work that one expects to see in the centre of a table among the salt cellars and trophies at a City banquet, enlarged into a building nearly 200 feet high.

Imperial Splendours

Despite this, the Memorial was designed by a man who understood the importance of skyline in our usually grey climate. Its outline is intricate and three-dimensional. It changes as you walk round it. In sunlight it shines like a flame over the billowing trees of Kensington Gardens. It is a foil to the spire (also by Sir Gilbert Scott) of St Mary Abbot's Church, Kensington. It dominates the axis of the museum land which flows south of it: another Victorian conception.

That area is now dulled by London University, but the memorial tower (1887–93) of Thomas Collcutt's splendid Imperial institute has been allowed to remain, happy and glorious.

The mortal remains of the Prince Consort lie beside his queen in a classical mausoleum in the garden of Frogmore, a country house in Windsor. It is really from mausolea, temples, and pillars in the parks of big country houses that post-Reformation public memorials in Britain originate, with the single exception of Wren's Monument to the Great Fire of London (1666) in the City. But this was part of a plan of wide streets and vistas which came to nothing.

On the Continent there was much town building in the grand classical manner in the seventeenth and eighteenth centuries and monuments were put up to terminate straight vistas or form the centrepiece of a square. In these islands, with the exception of places like Bath, Edinburgh, Cheltenham and Dublin, our older towns are mostly places of winding streets which do not lend themselves to this sort of adornment.

So our earliest public memorials (except for those in churches and churchyards) are in the landscaped parks of country houses. The finest of all is the circular temple mausoleum by Nicholas Hawksmoor in the grounds of Castle Howard, Yorkshire. Broad stone steps lead up to the colonnade, but there is no gap between the columns to mark the entrance, for nobody would willingly enter a house of death before he need.

Another splendid mausoleum is that to the Pelham family in the park of Brocklesby, Lincolnshire. It is a domed circular temple. One looks down from a gallery into a circular space, in whose wall are doors to the vaults. At West Wycombe, in Buckinghamshire, the strange mausoleum of the Dashwood family tops the hill beside the church and can be seen from High Wycombe. In its walls are niches for urns, intended to hold human hearts.

Not all such monuments in Georgian parks are mausolea. Very often a landowner would want to put up a column as an eye-catcher to be seen from the windows of his house and then would give it the name of some distinguished person. Coke of Norfolk is thus commemorated at Holkham; George III's recovery from illness is remembered on the column in Savernake Forest, Wiltshire. There are many other examples.

Ancestral Columns

These columns are the ancestors of things like Lord Nelson's column in Trafalgar Square, and the Duke of York's in Carlton House Terrace, the George IV column in Devonport, the Grey Column in Newcastle upon Tyne, and the Smelt column in Castletown, the old capital of the Isle of Man.

These columns in towns were, apart from statues, our first secular architectural monuments in public places. The taste for Gothic in Victorian times called a halt to what was considered a pagan form of memorial. People looked for mediaeval public monuments and, apart from cathedrals and churches, could find only market crosses and the crosses which had been put up to mark the halting places of the body of Queen Eleanor of Castile, wife of Edward I, on its journey from Nottinghamshire to London, as suitable examples.

The Martyrs' Memorial in Oxford, by Sir Gilbert Scott (1841) is one of the first Gothic Revival monuments in our streets. Charing Cross, on the site of an old Eleanor Cross, in front of the station, is another. It was designed by Sir E.M. Barry in 1864, and is now encrusted with pigeon dung. The Scott monument at Edinburgh and the Albert Memorial, which form steepled canopies over their statues, are derived from market crosses like the fifteenth century cross in the square of Leighton Buzzard in Bedfordshire, as much as from mediaeval reliquaries.

Dome Extraordinary

Public monuments of the Gothic Revival petered out in Britain in a plethora of clock towers. These were thought of, not as terminations to a vista, but as romantic outlines and objects of public use. One of the most elegant and original is Edgar Wood's Art Nouveau Gothic clock tower in Lindley, a suburb of Huddersfield.

In Edwardian times, there was the reaction against Gothic, but it was difficult to create long vistas for classical monuments in our overcrowded towns. The Queen Victoria monument at the end of the Mall, with sculpture by Brock (1901) and layout by Sir Aston Webb is the best known. It is neither so vast and ornate as the Victor Emmanuel Monument (1885–1911) in Rome, nor so satisfying as the Taj Mahal (1630–48).

The most extraordinary Edwardian public memorial is the Williamson Park and Mausoleum outside Lancaster. This is in full-blown Edwardian Renaissance by the Irvingite architect, John Belcher and was finished in 1907. Winding walks of flowers and evergreens climb past palm houses to the enormous domed mausoleum of the first wife of Lord Ashton. He had made a fortune in linoleum. In its setting, this great domed building seems as large as St Paul's.

Living Memorials

The finest Edwardian memorial landscaping is undoubtedly the city centre of Cardiff and this is chiefly due to the architects, Lanchester and Rickards and Dunbar Smith and Brewer. They turned open space given by Lord Bute in the middle of Cardiff into the noblest city centre in Great Britain. In the middle of it is the Welsh War Memorial in classic style by Sir Ninian Comper.

The 1914 war seems to have knocked the heart out of memorial architecture. The grim and impressive simplicity of Sir Edwin Lutyens' Cenotaph in Whitehall seems to say: 'This is the end of civic splendour and public ostentation. Too many lives have been lost. Things are more serious.'

Except for Sir Edward Maufe's RAF memorial at Runnymede, we do not seem to have gone in very much since then for this sort of architecture. Even the Skylon in the 1951 Exhibition was taken away. Instead we subscribe to social work and cancer research. Public memorials are the expression of an age. It will be interesting to see the design for the proposed memorial plinth to President Kennedy at Runnymede.

Must it go?
Sundry Articles on
Architecture

☙ ❧

Less than a year after joining the *Telegraph* as a fiction reviewer, perhaps inevitably, Betjeman graduated to the comment pages with an architectural article criticising Sir Basil Spence's design for Coventry Cathedral in no uncertain terms. Come early 1952 and he was bylined as the newspaper's architectural correspondent, although given the infrequency of articles written by him under this moniker one wonders just how much of an honorific title it actually was. Early on it was more a spur for polemical pieces, usually about the preservation of worthy buildings of the past and condemnation of modern developments which were not to his taste (indeed the title of this book comes from the headline of one of these early articles). However, his later writings as architectural correspondent would be more in the nature of reportage, such as a eulogy on the death of Giles Gilbert Scott in 1960.

After the 'Betjeman's Britain' series petered out in the mid-sixties he continued to pop up from time to time in the magazine with more architectural articles, and it was here that he would write a signature piece about preserving St Pancras station, at a time when certain people were intent on its demolition – a campaign of his which would eventually have a happy outcome. Come 1970 and magazine readers were presented with a major twelve-part series titled 'Periods of Architecture' (not reprinted here as it did not make sense to take just one or two articles out of this series) which spanned prehistoric times to the modern age and was later reprinted in book form. For over two decades *Telegraph* readers were treated to a variety of articles on an architectural theme by John Betjeman; here are the major ones from this time.

Design for a New Cathedral

3 September 1951

෯Ⓒ೮

S ome people still think of a cathedral as the local church, only more so. The altar is further away, the stained-glass windows are bigger, the services are longer and the choir is a bit better. Otherwise it is the same as an ordinary 'church' with rather more people there and the sermon booming away through amplifiers hung like homemade wireless sets on the mighty columns of the nave.

Nothing could be further from the mediaeval purpose of a cathedral. It was never intended for a gigantic preaching place. Indeed, the public were not encouraged, except as lucrative pilgrims to shrines. The monks said masses at many altars in the early morning. These services went on in different parts of the building at the same time. Monks gathered for their daily offices in the choir, as the dean and canons still do in the choirs of our old cathedrals. Our great buildings were for the most part monastic.

In considering Mr Spence's design for the new Coventry Cathedral we must remember, before any preoccupation with style, the purpose of a cathedral, and St Michael's, Coventry, was never built as such. It was a town church raised to the status of cathedral in the present century.

A People's Church

In the Middle Ages it had been a people's church, built and added to by the citizens of Coventry themselves. The girdlers, dyers, drapers, cappers and mercers had each built themselves chapels on to the church. They maintained the lights, gave the vestments, jewels and stained glass, ironwork and woodwork and paid their own priests. The butchers and marlers and other religious guilds built chapels on to Holy Trinity Church next door.

The devotion of these tough and unemotional merchants and craftsmen is one of the shining jewels of mediaeval religion. They may have mingled superstition with their prayers to patron saints but they gave of their best to their churches.

Mr Spence and the people who defined the rules of the competition were going back to the old tradition in wanting a building which was to represent Coventry. It would be no bad thing if the Christians employed by the motor, the bicycle and other great industries of Coventry each maintained a chapel in the new cathedral.

But such is not to be. The new design does not allow for more than three altars besides the main one. Great stress was laid on the provision of a Chapel of Unity where Nonconformists (excluding Roman Catholics) and our own Church might meet. Mr Spence has solved this problem very cleverly.

The ruined cathedral, like English churches almost without exception, had its altar at the east end. The new building is at right angles to the older cathedral and with its altar facing north. The ruins are to be retained and turned into a 'Garden of Rest', that is to say one of those places with municipal lawns where you are not quite sure whether it is sacrilegious to eat a lunch among the rather over-preserved remains.

From the ruins it will be possible to glimpse through a series of glass screens the altar of the cathedral, which is below a blank wall hung with what will be the largest piece of tapestry in the world and not yet designed. The side walls of the new cathedral are a zigzag formation with windows shining towards the altar and therefore, when you are inside the building, and looking towards the altar, invisible.

These zigzags are to contain something never heard of before called 'hallowing places'. Above them will be symbolical sculpture. One is roughly outlined in Mr Spence's designs. It shows 'Agriculture', a man in trousers digging a furrow, a symbolic tree, a mediaeval man below it and an angel in the sky.

Are worshippers meant to drop down on their knees in the 'hallowing place' – a shelf is provided and there is room for a chair or two – and say a prayer to Agriculture – 'O blessed Agriculture …?' Or, in some other zigzag, to start 'I beseech thee, holy Civics …?' Surely such worship and such symbolism are a little remote and cold even for today?

The walls of this great hall are too of the lovely pinkish-grey local stone, both without and within. The thin pillars which support the shallow concrete vault are to be steel encased with concrete.

Finely Conceived

The best feature of this new cathedral seems to me to be the west-east axis, that is to say the view across the building. This is all to do with the 'Chapel of Unity'. Mr Spence has designed it as a star shape against his west wall, out of sight of the high altar but looking straight across to the font and main entrance. This is finely conceived.

But what is a 'Chapel of Unity'? It has no altar. Is it a place where we each agree to give up something which our church holds sacred for the sake of getting on with another church? The result is surely a decreased creed for each of us just in order to be in the same room together on this earth. I am reminded of Gabriel Gillett's lines:

> See all from all men's point of
> view; use others' eyes to see with;
> And never preach what anyone
> could ever disagree with.

Mr Spence himself is an architect of imagination and with a sense of detail as well as plan, as his Sea and Ships Pavilion on the South Bank and this cathedral fully testify. The good points of his design are the happy relation of the stern masses of his new building with the elegant thin ruins.

Effective Contrast

The skyline is also carefully considered. His new buildings act as a contrasting solid to the soaring spire and pinnacles of the old church. His plan is ingenious and grows on one.

His revival of the use of local stone is to be praised and it is to hoped that when he comes to use this stone he will dispense with the affectation of having no mouldings. For mouldings are essential to throwing up the beauty and purpose of stonework as paint is to the body of a motor car.

But the building seems to me to be a failure because it is not a cathedral but a secular assembly hall with a font against one wall and an altar against another. The nave is too wide, the aisles are too narrow and too much depends on the artist who is chosen to design the huge tapestry above the high altar. The altar itself is too far away.

It lacks mystery and the endlessness of vista upon vista characteristic of our faith itself. Compare it with Pearson's fine modern cathedral of Truro. It also lacks the rock-like look of Scott's Liverpool Cathedral. It is far below the original genius of Burges's Cathedral of St Finbar, Cork. It does not pray as a church should. Instead, it surprises like an exhibition building.

Wrong Conditions Set

I do not think this is all the fault of Mr Spence but of the people who set the conditions of the competition. They were so anxious that the building should be all things to all men that it expresses not a firm faith but a woolly goodwill. There is all the difference between being kind and believing something.

Our Church of England is a sacramental Church. We claim that it has Apostolic succession. We stress the sacraments of Baptism and Holy Communion. Many of us use the other sacraments which are available in our Church. We are a unity in ourselves. We have Protestants and Catholics among us. Our teaching is in our catechism and Prayer Book. Many millions have died in it.

The cathedral should be a strong hold of our faith. But this building is too much an auditorium, too suggestive of an impracticable compromise, and we all know where compromise can lead us. Indeed, one of the 219 competitors, presumably aware of this, designed his cathedral wholly underground.

***

Concrete Lamp Standards in Old Town Settings

23 February 1952

ဆၢ

N one will deny the need for good street lighting. But there is growing concern about the ugly concrete lamp standards which are being introduced into our old streets and country towns.

The Minister of Transport requires lights along trunk roads to be over a certain height and at a certain distance apart. What type of standard is used is left to the local authorities, but the Minister pays a percentage of the cost if the local authorities use a design which has been passed by the Royal Fine Art Commission.

The Council's surveyor will produce a sheaf of catalogues with which he has been supplied. On some of these concrete firms supplying the designs put 'Passed by the Royal Fine Art Commission'.

It is not until the standards are up that bewildered citizens and possibly members of the street lighting committee itself realise that the Royal Fine Art Commission could not possibly have approved of these towering sick serpents which have wholly altered the skyline and scale and look of the town. And they will be right, for the Royal Fine Art Commission does not approve of the placing of these concrete standards in old towns.

In August 1950, Lord Crawford, the chairman of the Royal Fine Art Commission, stated the position of the Commission.

> The standards now being erected throughout the country have caused the Commission much concern. Of the many designs submitted for them, few have met with approval ... The Commission has confined its activities to 'passing' those who avoided the worst faults ...
>
> But even if standards are well designed for trunk-roads, they may look grotesque in different surroundings. The siting material and size of new standards are as important as their design ... Far more consideration should be given to the matter, especially when it is essential to provide new installations in old settings.

The Commission could not have approved of the examples illustrated here, nor of other such schemes all over the country of which Banbury, Abingdon, Devizes, Crewkerne, Wantage, Lincoln, Corsham, Carlisle and Wokingham are only some horrible examples known to me personally.

At the present moment Marlborough's famous High Street is threatened with a line of concrete standards down either side and another row down the middle. It is a pity that the Royal Fine Art Commission ever allowed itself to get into a position where its name could be used to encourage such brutalisation.

If you start to look at old iron lamp-posts in side streets, especially those which have not been altered by 'swan-necks' in place of their original glass lanterns, you will see how gracefully they fit into any street. Their proportions date from late Georgian times. They vary from district to district, as does everything good and traditional in England.

Concrete standards never vary except in brutality. They lack proportion in themselves and to their surroundings. A very thick column generally of lumpy shape with a giant's match-strike at its base rears up to bend over and carry, one would expect, a very large corpse. Instead, all this effort goes into hanging a tiny bubble of a light or else a thing like a carpet sweeper.

Concrete will never weather; it will only streak and crack. It is too thick at its base for the narrow pavements of old towns, too unyielding in its texture beside the infinite and delicate varieties of building materials all over England, too coarse in its detail and outline beside the subtle mouldings and carvings which survive in almost every English town.

The chief argument in its favour is that it is cheap and easily obtainable. But we should not sacrifice the priceless heritage of our modest and easily damaged town architecture to such a penny wise, pound foolish policy.

There are alternatives. Where the houses are tall enough – and that is in most towns – Newbury's example can be followed. Here simple iron brackets have been fixed to the upper storeys of the houses.

In daytime they lose themselves in the hanging signs of the main street. At night they shed an ample white light. Bath has similar lighting. There is no compulsion to have that blue or orange light which drains the colour from old brick and the blood from our faces.

Where the surrounding houses are too low, iron standards, as at Swindon and Oxford, are preferable. And if the shortage of steel is so great now that not even for such beautiful places as, let us say, Ludlow, Louth, Oundle, Stratford-upon-Avon, Cheltenham, Bristol, Newcastle, Wells, King's Lynn or Reepham is steel permissible, then even wooden poles will do as a temporary measure.

Every lighting authority will be doing England a service if before embarking on a scheme it consults the local representative of a body like the Council for the Preservation of Rural England. This can be arranged by direct contact with the London headquarters of the CPRE. And in big towns the local Arts or Architecture Society could give advice.

A town may be beautified by a well-thought-out lighting scheme. England's beauty is in its variety and it is ours to protect. Each place is a different problem.

***

The Churches of England are Part of Our Life

30 May 1952

&oCG

There are 15,779 churches in England alone. This excludes Nonconformist, Roman Catholic and other places of worship. Of this total more than 8,000 are mediaeval.

The village church is usually the history of a parish in stone, wood and glass since Norman times.

Flint of East Anglia, ragstone of Kent, chalk of Wilts, red sandstone of Devon, golden limestone of the Cotswolds, silver granite of Cornwall, brown ironstone of north Oxfordshire, grey or green stones of the North, pink of Warwickshire, half-timber of Hereford and Shropshire; towers in Norfolk and Suffolk and Somerset, spires in Northampton and Rutland and Lincs – it is a huge inheritance, far less damaged by civil strife than the churches of anywhere else in Europe.

And think of the interiors, sun coming through clear glass on to sculptured monuments, box pews or pitch-pine pews, old stone floors or shiny Victorian ones, cow parsley in the brass altar vases in May, honesty in winter, Hymns A & M or English Hymnal according to the 'height' of the vicar, timbered roofs and stained-glass windows, cool stone arches and the fluttering statements of last week's collections pinned to the notice board in the porch.

Great Victorians

Again, there is the stately town church built after the manner of Wren, with a mayor's pew and sword rests and a west gallery with huge gold-piped organ in carved cedar wood case.

There are the noble Victorian churches by such great architects as Pearson, Butterfield and Street, in seaside towns and industrial suburbs, where lengthened nave and lofty chancel lead the eye to a rich altar and stately ceremonial. There are the little brick mission churches of little brick streets, and the evangelical hymn-singing interiors of the North.

There are the great mediaeval fabrics which rise to architecture – Patrington, Yorks; Ottery St Mary, Devon; Thaxted, Essex; Boston, Lincs; Walpole St Peter, Norfolk; Lavenham, Suffolk; Edington, Wilts, to name six out of as many hundreds.

Beyond Parish Means

The churches of England are not museums, they are part of our life. Those of us who use them week by week love them; those millions who only go inside them for baptisms, weddings and funerals love them too; the agnostic and the old-fashioned atheist, though they may snort at the faith which built and has kept the churches, will admit their beauty.

Church bells ring through our literature; the lovely Prayer Book English colours our language. Artists like Hogarth, Turner, Cotman and Constable have painted churches; pavement artists depict them, and even the drop curtain of a variety theatre will show a church spire peeping over the painted elms. Our churches are so much part of us that we sometimes forget they are there.

The report of a Commission of the Church Assembly published today by the Church Information Board, Church House, Dean's Yard, London, SW1, price 5s., shows that over 3,000 of these precious buildings, nearly all of them mediaeval, are in need of repair. More than 2,000 have repair bills greater than their parishes can possibly pay. These are mostly in districts with large churches in villages no longer populous.

There are 269 churches needing repairs between £2,000 and £3,000; 123 need more than £5,000 worth of repairs each. The total sum which the Commission estimates must be found in the next ten years to supplement the efforts of parishes is £4 million.

The annual repair bill thereafter should be £750,000, which should be within the means of the churches.

Until now the Church has been able to keep its buildings in repair. People will immediately connect this enormous bill with the decline in church worship. But that is not the cause. Church worship has gone up in quality.

Local Generosity

People go to church today not because it is respectable, but because they believe or want to believe and live the Christian life. They give generously, but the richer people who used to give much to churches have been taxed out of their incomes.

Let me quote two instances of how parishes have helped their churches in the last few months. To repair the great town church of St Alfege in Greenwich, which is by no means a rich district, £9,000 is needed. In six months the parish itself gave £1,000.

For the little village church of Iwerne Minster in Dorset £5,000 is wanted. In nine months this parish of about 500 people, none of them rich, raised £1,000. The Methodists in the village gave £100, which is true Christian charity.

These are but two instances of hundreds, and I could quote many others. But the money raised locally is nothing like enough.

Then there are enormous churches like Holy Trinity, Hull, that miracle of Perpendicular architecture in a city almost as rich as Bristol in beautiful buildings; £900 a year is needed to help to keep it up. On top of this, Holy Trinity must find another £12,000 at once to prevent the fabric collapsing altogether.

Arrears Due to the War

The delay in repair work during and after the war is the chief cause of the sudden expenses. Bomb damage to churches is partially paid for by the War Damage Commission. But time damages an old building as effectively as bombs. Gutters have to be kept clear, interiors heated and ventilated, small repairs carried out before they become big repairs.

From 1940 it was not possible to carry out any substantial repairs without a licence. Even if the licence could be obtained scarcity of labour and raw materials made repairs impossible. So the Church is faced with a bill for ten years of neglect imposed by the necessities of the State, and it possesses buildings more vulnerable to neglect than those of any other body in the country.

In 1950 the Church spent £1½ million of accumulated funds on repair work; £4 million more is needed. The Church hopes not to have to go to the State for this money. It might well meet with a rebuff or with some sort of bargain that might interfere with its teaching and practice.

The inspiring and lucid report of the Commission under the chairmanship of Mr Ivor Bulmer-Thomas proposes, among other things, the formation of a Trust for the Preservation of Historic Churches, appointed by the Archbishops of Canterbury and York.

Spiritual Capital

County trusts should be created to help the central fund. Every parish should keep a repair and restoration fund distinct from its other accounts. The appeal should be on a national scale, but through their local branches subscribers will be able to earmark money for particular churches.

Next Sunday over elm trees and thatch, over town streets and silent factories, over meadows and downs, moors and hills, the bells will be ringing for 'high', 'low' or 'broad' services of the Church of England. Whatever your opinion of the vicar, whatever your views on religion, those towers and churches will not be standing much longer if we cannot find the £4 million needed to preserve them.

A civilisation is remembered by its buildings. Maybe all that future ages will find of our great civilisation will be the ruins of chain stores and concrete lamp standards. But the £4 million is a cross that most of us will be honoured to carry, and perhaps we shall induce others who had thought of doing so to help us to carry it. England is full of charity. It is part of the spiritual capital with which for centuries our churches have provided us.

***

Lovely Bits of Old England
Must be Spared

26 July 1952

୫୦ ଓଃ

The Middlesex county planners are proposing to destroy an attractive part of the old Thames-side village of Twickenham. Other plans for other counties are in preparation, and we must be prepared for more destruction.

Some planners, but by no means all, thank goodness, look at places from the height of an aeroplane and think in terms of maps and figures. They give too much priority to lorries, clinics and community centres.

They do not live and have gardens and little family houses in the places they plan. The worst of them want to turn us from a nation of house dwellers into a nation of flat dwellers living in huge hygienic Karl Marx Hofs, ants in an insect world of the future.

They have employed an army of pedants to list buildings of 'historical or architectural interest', and some of these buildings will be left, dead and pointless, like furniture in a museum, among their blocks of flats.

Town-Minded Planners

Such buildings are part of the lip service which the worst planners pay to what they call 'amenities', an item which is low on their lists. By amenities they also mean open spaces in areas where farming may be done. They are almost all town-minded men. They live in a world of theory.

We who love England, its infinitely varied scenery, changing from county to county with different vegetation and building materials, each have one part of it we call home. If we live in intolerable conditions, we hope, at any rate, for some house of our dreams. It may not be of 'first-class architectural importance' but it will be England for us.

If it is in the country, it may be known by the turn of a lane, a group of trees, the shapes of fields and hills, a public house on a corner, a church, however Victorianised, or a brick chapel, and the old village cottages and shops.

If it is a town, it may be a street of bow-windowed houses with privet hedges and squeaking iron gates and a small back garden, and a glimpse of some truncated Victorian spire above the chimney pots.

Splendid Craftsmanship

No one wants slums. But old country cottages can be repaired and enlarged for less than the cost of building new ones, if only the local authorities will give us a licence for repairs.

And in towns street life is happier for a family than the anonymous life of flats, however sumptuous the lift and entrance hall. And not very much more space is taken up.

England, of any country in Europe, has the best domestic architecture, for our civil war came before our great period of house building. And we have a long tradition of good craftsmanship.

Think of the tile-hung and brick cottages of Kent, the stone-mullioned cottages of Gloucestershire, Rutland and

Northamptonshire, the timber-framed houses of Shropshire and Cheshire, the reed-thatched and plastered cottages of East Anglia, the weatherboarded inns of Essex, the red-tiled and pale pink-walled old houses of Yorkshire, the low storm-resisting stone houses of the Lake District, the granite of Cornwall, the cob-walled cottages of Devon, the stucco terraces of the spas and older seaside towns.

Think of the fine lettering still to be seen over some shops and on country farm carts and in the names of streets in places like Louth and Bath.

Notice how the stone tiles and slates of old houses are graded, small at the ridge and getting larger to the eaves. Notice how windows are related to wall space, large on the ground or first floor, smaller on the higher floors.

Worship of Speed

Notice, too, how old bricks are smaller than new ones, how in counties like Kent, Lincolnshire, Berkshire and Middlesex the old bricks are varied in texture and colour and arranged in decorative patterns on Georgian houses and how some retain the light and glow like smouldering fire. Notice how in every old house there are mouldings round doors and chimney pieces.

Notice different styles in different districts of doing chimney stacks, window glazing, painting, weather proofing. Not all of it is 'important', but it is local, modest and done with a love of craftsmanship which has lasted for centuries. We should miss it if it were not there.

Above all, notice how old buildings group themselves together, and how, if you take one away, you affect the whole group.

Anyone can enjoy architecture. It is a public gallery always open, and which we can all see if we use our eyes. Architecture — and that includes the setting of a building — is the enduring record of a civilisation. And we are destroying it as fast as we can.

There are some very good living architects. But we dread the look of new buildings, because they are too often out of scale and out of texture with any old ones near them. And beauty is much concerned with proportion and texture.

Today almost all bricks are the same colour and size, and all windows of the same non-sash metal type which looks hideous in old buildings or near them. Roofing material is standardised. Cement is used instead of lime, concrete instead of wood or iron. We worship cheapness and speed. Our best new building is all brain and no heart or reverence.

Twickenham Houses

Let me end where I started, with the proposed destruction of part of old Twickenham. One house, Strand House, is to be left, because it is on a list. The rest are to be replaced by flats.

Yet the point of this house is that it is part of a group. There is no ugly building near it, and yet there is only one other building which an 'expert' would list. It is just a happy cluster of old roofs, varied local brick houses and little lanes, and a beautifully curved Georgian street descending to the church. There is also a riverside inn.

As many people could be housed on the site if some of the old buildings were repaired as could live in flats. And there they would live, protected from the weather, in quiet and in small houses of their own. It might cost almost as much as the demolition of the old village and building the new flats.

But the planners have labelled this part of Twickenham 'obsolete' and so it must go.

Defying the Theorists

Must it go? All over England we are becoming aware of the threat to our trees and buildings. Local preservation societies are springing up. There are larger organisations like the Council for the Preservation of Rural England, the Society for the Protection of Ancient Buildings, the Georgian Group. They can find architects who will look at property with the idea of preserving it while making it habitable, instead of destroying it. Only by supporting such societies and keeping them informed can we hope to preserve places we like against soulless theorists in county councils and State departments.

***

Architecture of the Conquerors

14 January 1966

ഇൗൽ

I t is hard to imagine how England must have looked to the Saxons and Normans. Roads were grassy tracks, often along the tops of the hills. Here and there the straight roads engineered by the Romans survived, covered with weeds. There were many square miles of forest and scrub, with wild boar in them. Rivers were a chief means of transport. Nature predominated over man. Villages were clearings in the marsh or scrub where there was drinking water from wells.

Twilight must have been an alarming time. You never knew what wild beast or armed enemy might suddenly appear. I fancy that the strange creatures one sometimes sees carved in Norman churches, particularly on the Celtic borders, as at Kilpeck, Herefordshire, were reminiscences of these.

Magic was in the air. The place for spiritual safety was the church. Many Norman churches were like fortified buildings, with little windows and thick walls. The place for bodily safety was the baron's castle or the abbey.

By the time the Normans came, the Saxons were a civilised agricultural people. They were delicate artists, as can be seen from the Lindisfarne Gospel, now in the British Museum. They knew more about architectural construction than the Normans, though they often built in wood. Where their stone buildings survive, as at Brixworth in Northants, and the crypt at Repton, Derbyshire, they create a sense of space and elegance more impressive than many much larger Norman buildings.

So far as style is concerned, there was not all that much difference between late Saxon and early Norman architecture. Both used the round arches of the Romanesque manner, found then in Christian churches all over Europe.

William the Conqueror and his Norman followers changed the look of England by their buildings. They used them to placate and impress Saxons and Celts. They built themselves castles at strategic points – on the banks of rivers, as at Rochester and London, and on view-commanding eminences. They built a keep with immense walls to withstand all the known devices for attack. The ground floor was dark, with small windows just for letting in air.

The entrance was on the first floor, and approached by a movable ladder or a stone staircase built into a well-defended tower. On the first floor the inhabitants ate and slept, except for the baron, who, with his family, lived on the floor above. And on the top floor were battlements for active defence.

The keep was surrounded by walled courtyards. Castle keeps were of various shapes, round as at Windsor, square as at Castle Hedingham, or mightily buttressed as at Conisborough, Yorkshire.

Most Norman castles are ruins, because, as the country grew more peaceful, they were no longer necessary and the inhabitants moved out into the villages. If you want to get an idea of what a castle was like, the best example I know is Castell Coch, outside Cardiff, restored by William Burges in 1875.

The other great buildings which the Normans put up were abbeys, and they made them particularly grand and enormous where the Saxons were inclined to be rebellious, as in East Anglia, or near the Welsh, or up in the disaffected North at Durham.

The Normans went in for size. The taller they made their walls, the thicker the walls had to be; and they were not very good at laying foundations. On a night in February 1322, the central tower of Ely Cathedral fell, and the result was the greatest Gothic lantern in the world, built to replace it.

Then there was the problem of roofing these huge buildings. The Normans were able to construct stone vaults over square spaces in the aisles of their abbeys, but over the huge naves they put wooden roofs. A chief cause of the pointed arch and the Gothic style was the necessity of roofing an oblong space with stone. This could only be done by pinching up the narrower arch to the same height as the top of the broader arch on either side of the oblong. In this country this was first done at Durham.

Almost every mediaeval church in England has Norman remains. The Normans kept the divisions of parishes of the Saxons, and the boundaries of country parishes are still generally streams. But the Normans rebuilt the village churches in their Romanesque style, with round arches, thick walls, small windows high up and with deep splays, a round chancel arch and a rounded east end, called an apse. The English fashion had been to have a square end, and village churches some distance from France were built with square ends even in Norman times. The little stones which formed the arches were carved with patterns, very often zigzag, there was another ornamental layer below with another pattern, and sculptured columns supporting the arch. The plan was often either nave, chancel, arch and chancel, or sometimes a tower between nave and chancel and therefore two arches. Larger churches were cross-shaped.

Inside, the walls were plastered and painted with squares and sometimes with pictures of saints in window splays. The prevailing colours were cream and light red. Stained glass was a luxury. People were not able to make large pieces of glass, so there was much leading in windows. The glass was thick and the main colours rich red and deep blue.

Finally, when we think of Norman England, we must not think of England being conscious of itself as a separate country. England and France were part of Western Christendom, and where they were near to each other, along the south coast of England and the northern coast of France, there is a great similarity in the churches.

Church and State – if the Normans did not invent the idea, their buildings embody it, and the emphasis is on Church.

***

Temple to the Age of Steam

11 November 1966

ໂດ໌ ໃຊ

T o some people St Pancras is just an old station which may be replaced. To others it is an irreplaceable example of the exuberant architecture of the 1860s, when British engineers, railways and business led the world.

In England, St Pancras is less known as a Roman boy martyr than as a London railway station. Even the former borough, and the old and new parish churches from which it took its name, are less in the public mind than that romantic cluster of towers and gables which still dominates King's Cross and district. The roof over the station itself, finished in 1868, remained for nearly a century the largest roof in the world without any interior support.

Like the Albert Memorial, St Pancras Hotel – by the same architect – and station are coming into their own. This is partly because of the perspective the passage of time gives us. A century ago, most people thought the Georgian style we now so much admire heathen and meretricious. Places like Bath and palaces like Blenheim were considered repetitive and ostentatious.

Even shortly after it was finished, there was one critic who castigated the Gothic hotel at St Pancras as incorrect, because he was the sort of mediaevalist who thought everything ought to be hand-made by masons working under monks. But most people thought St Pancras the finest building in London.

In the priggish 1930s, critics allowed us to admire the station roof. Now we are beginning to see the merits of the hotel as well. It stands as a monument to the great age of steam power and mid-Victorian self-confidence, when Britain was top nation in the world. As David Piper has said in his recent *Companion Guide to London*: 'Its value to the skyline is inestimable, even more so as the rigour of concrete and glass envelops more and more of London.' But under a British Rail plan to amalgamate St Pancras and King's Cross stations into a single modern terminus, the station and hotel are threatened with destruction and replacement by another series of biscuit boxes. Neither building is listed by the Ministry of Public Building and Works. Yet since the Doric portico at Euston – the first grand entrance to the first trunk railway in the world – was demolished, despite the offer of Mr Valori, the demolisher, to number the stones and keep them at his own expense till the portico could be re-erected on another site, there is no monument in London to the railway age comparable with St Pancras. Euston's granite has been ground to powder.

In Victorian times, the provinces were champing to reach London. The Great Western Railway was largely a Bristol project. The Midland Railway, an amalgamation of companies, had its headquarters in Derby. It had running powers to London reluctantly granted to it for a large sum, first to Euston and later, using the Great Northern's line, to King's Cross. At last in 1863 it constructed its own line to London from Bedford, and was meant to connect with the newly opened steam underground railway between Paddington and the City. A few forgotten trains – two a day – still carry passengers in the rush hours between Moorgate Street Station and the Midland main line through a tunnel which passes under St Pancras and comes up near Kentish Town.

The engineer of the great train shed of St Pancras Station was W.H. Barlow (1812–1902), the Midland's resident engineer who completed it in 1868. He invented new systems of signalling and also made experiments with waves of sound which led to the discovery of the telephone and the gramophone. He was assisted by R.M. Ordish, who had worked on the Crystal Palace, and who designed the Albert Suspension Bridge over the Thames to Battersea Park. What was wanted for the trains was as wide a span of roof as possible, and no interrupting columns.

Now it so happened that the Midland was not just a passenger line; its goods traffic was equally important, and the brewers of Burton-on-Trent wanted a London store for their barrels of beer. So Barlow combined station and storehouse in one of the most brilliant feats of engineering of the last century. He made the roof of ribs of cast-iron bent round and held together by tie beams, so that no internal support was needed for its 240-foot span of cast iron and glass. It is really like a series of tightly strung longbows, placed parallel on the top of brick vaults which stored the beer, and the trains run over these, and the tie beams.

To relieve tension caused by expansion and contraction of the iron in different weathers, Barlow snapped the bow at its apex, so that the roof goes to a slight point. The station was built for fifty trains a day and is still adequate for more than thrice that number. Its only disadvantages are that the space behind the buffers is too narrow for crowds in rush hours and the platforms are too short for some long modern trains.

Sir Gilbert Scott, then at the top of the architectural profession, won the competition for the hotel in 1865. It was built when the train shed was complete.

Professor Pevsner has scotched the legend that the St Pancras Hotel was Scott's Gothic design for the Foreign Office in Whitehall, which Palmerston had rejected ten years before, but this lying legend persists. As a matter of fact, Scott had long been building large houses in the Gothic style — witness Kelham in Nottinghamshire, and his Broad Sanctuary buildings at right angles to the west end of Westminster Abbey. His Midland Hotel design bears no resemblance to the Foreign Office design either in plan or elevation.

It was built when railway companies erected hotels across the fronts of their London termini, as had already been done at Paddington, Charing Cross and Cannon Street. The ground floor was mostly used for station rooms and offices, and arched exits and entrances to the station and the hotel proper started on the first floor.

The building was finished in 1872, and was far the most sumptuous hotel in London, with accommodation for 600 guests. It had, even then, electric bells and hydraulic lifts. Here the Midland businessman had his own castle, as romantic inside as it is outside, and proclaiming the power of 'brass'. An immense Gothic porch on the Euston Road leads by shallow steps to the main staircase running almost the whole height of the hotel, with its cast-iron and stone vaulting. The same carpet that was woven for this stair is still in use and not at all threadbare. No details are skimped. The outside of the hotel is of specially made Nottingham brick, the bands of stone are also from the north Midlands. Splendid fireplaces, tiled rooms and well-made doors survive. The vaulted passages are like a cathedral, and the views from the windows are unexampled.

The building ceased to be an hotel in 1935, and is partitioned rather cruelly into offices. So well built are station and hotel that they survived several hits from bombs and were easily repaired.

A history of St Pancras Station is being written by Professor Jack Simmons, and he once said of it in a lecture: 'Like all great buildings it has a personality, strong and peculiar to itself. For my part I seize it most clearly coming into the vast shed on a sunny morning, the early light streaming in to pull out the powerful repeated curves of the girders, the fiery red of the interior walls;

and in the evening, when the rich brickwork of the hotel glows crimson and its fantastic towers and pinnacles are lighted up by the sun from the west. Only the Houses of Parliament exercise the same kind of power on me. These two buildings are surely the quintessential expression in stone and brick of the romantic spirit of nineteenth-century England.'

More damage has been done to London and our other old towns by 'developers' and their tame architects than ever was done by German bombing. No one can object to the clearance of what is shoddy and badly built: St Pancras Station and its hotel, now called Midland Chambers, are neither. It is horrible to contemplate such careful work being destroyed to be replaced by what we are sure to be told is a masterpiece, but will all too probably be like every other new slab along the Euston Road. The Victorian Society is fighting to save St Pancras. Let us hope it will be saved, and a use found for the existing buildings. They would certainly make a worthy transport museum, instead of the present overcrowded premises in Clapham.

*****

Betjeman Goes Down the Strand

1 September 1967

೮೦ ೮ೞ

Palatial is the word for the Strand. It was a row of palaces and great houses on the north bank of the Thames between Charing Cross and the property of the Knights Templars (now the Temple, appropriated by lawyers). York House, Durham House, Cecil House, Savoy Palace – their names remain, and little alleys between the great blocks go down to the river between what once were their garden walls.

Only one palace survives, Somerset House. It was rebuilt in 1777 by Sir William Chambers for the Royal Academy and learned societies. Somerset House is now largely inhabited by Income Tax officials, and the square, which must be one of the finest in Europe, is their car park. The riverfront is cut off by the Victoria Embankment, 1864–70. We can only imagine how splendid these Strand buildings must have been when the Thames was wide and slow-flowing and full of fish and many-coloured craft.

Walk from Trafalgar Square to St Paul's. First there is that attempt made by the Strand to draw people away from Regent Street and Piccadilly Circus – the charming stucco building of the 1830s with its twin cupolas. Eastwards the Strand is less formal – the theatres, bars and little houses on the north side make it like any old high street. Opposite is the formidable bulk of what used to be the Cecil Hotel, and next to it what is still the Savoy, a grand 1880 building by T.F. Collcutt.

The most brilliant new building on this walk to St Paul's, if we exclude Somerset House, is the Law Courts by G.E. Street, built between 1868 and 1882. Notice how the design varies all the way along and is thought of as something to walk past and planned as a series of verticals.

Then everything narrows and we are approaching the once walled City of London. Even the press barons seem to be cowed, and their buildings are at least vertical. Wedged between them are the little offices of provincial papers, still trying to recall old London.

Ludgate Circus is nothing. The railway bridge kills the famous view of St Paul's across from the bottom of Ludgate Hill. This bridge has been made opaque when it used to be trellis. It is not until you reach the curve of Ludgate Hill itself that you see the subtlety of the West Front of Wren's St Paul's. He deliberately set it at an angle so that it should not look flat. He deliberately showed only one bell tower, and gave a hint of more to come. Since the war some fool has curved the building immediately before the building next to St Paul's – a lumpy piece of old world with-it-ry called Juxon House – so that there appears to be an unnatural projection. The prospect that Wren intended is ruined.

***

Greece, Rome and Hermits in the English Countryside

27 October 1967

☙ ❧

P eople in England have for centuries had a sense of landscape. If you go into the street of any village or town where there is an old church tower you will notice that the chief street curves so that two sides of the tower may be seen from it at once. This stops the tower looking flat.

Then have a look at any old street which has not been consciously planned and you will see how one house is flush with the pavement, another stands back, a garden wall is between one house and another, and how the houses themselves are of different shapes and materials and how differently the chimneys sit on the roofs. All this is what we have come to take for granted as the English village scene or town scene.

A great feature of the landscape or townscape is trees – a tree showing itself here or there between houses or in a churchyard. It was Thomas Sharp, the famous town planner, who first pointed out that just as important as any of the buildings which make the renowned curve of Oxford's High Street is the tree between All Souls and Queen's College on which everything else seems to focus. Yet probably whoever planted it wasn't consciously thinking of landscape at all.

Buildings in relation to landscape were thought of only subconsciously until Shakespeare's time and even later than that. There were no books about where to put houses or towers. We left that to the Italians and French, and then we suddenly began to think about it ourselves. People in the eighteenth century who had a bit of money and an estate in the country went on the Grand Tour and they saw the pictures painted by Claude Lorraine and his followers which showed ruined temples and castles on slopes of hills seen against the evening light. They brought back engravings and copies of them, and sometimes they bought the original paintings. They then looked at their own square fields with straight hedges, and formal straight gardens with clipped yew and box which had delighted the Elizabethans. These seemed old-fashioned and too stiff and too like tapestry. So they cut them all down and brought the park right up to the windows of the house and cut down the hedges and planted woods on the tops and slopes of hills so that there were no straight lines.

They wanted something to remind them of the Italian plains and distant mountains. If possible they put a temple or a column to be seen in the middle distance from the main rooms of the house so that they had an Italian picture or a French picture when they looked out of their windows to give verisimilitude to the Claudes and Poussins on their walls. They dammed up the stream until it looked like a lake and contrived a waterfall below the dam.

Later in the eighteenth century, when the mediaeval came into fashion, they even built a ruined castle to be seen from the house, or contrived a hermitage and dressed up a retainer as a hermit and put him to live in it when fashionable people came to call.

This was all right for the country. You were allowed curves there, because the famous landscape gardeners thought that nature abhorred a straight line. In towns, however, the straight line was *à la mode*, and each terrace in a town square was made to look like one big house with a lot of front doors in its chief façade. Queen's Square, Bath, and Grosvenor Square, London, were among the first of these.

At first they thought that streets should look like ancient Rome and should be straight and terminate in columns, obelisks or arches. Sir Christopher Wren wanted to redesign the City after the Fire of London in 1666 with straight roads radiating out in a sort of star from St Paul's Cathedral, but the citizens were so tenacious of the sites of their old houses and land was so valuable that he was not allowed to do this.

Instead, he concentrated on the skyline. There was a restriction imposed by which houses should not be higher than 60 feet. Thus he was able to create a forest of white Portland stone and black lead steeples sailing above the dark red-brick houses and leading the eye to the dome and cross of St Paul's, which then dominated the City and wide slow-flowing Thames.

In the next two centuries (in fact until about 1860) in new towns, particularly spas and watering places where there was money to be made out of elegant accommodation, new streets were wide and straight and generously planted. Often they had vistas at the end of distant hills so that you might feel that you were in ancient Rome or Greece. People despised the irregular and picturesque, except some of the more sophisticated. Thus came into being the New Town at Edinburgh, the finest of all our classic plans, Bath with its crescents and squares and parades; Clifton, Cheltenham, Newcastle and Liverpool; Regent's Park and Regent Street, London. The last of the great broadly planned inland schemes was Birkenhead. Many a town has the remains of a hoped-for Bath – Buxton, Melksham, Ashby-de-la-Zouch ...

Down by the sea, as soon as George III made sea-bathing fashionable and the sea ceased to be something uncouth and only suitable for sailors and fishermen, many a handsome watering place grew up – an Edinburgh New Town or a Bath-sur-Mer with the buildings in stucco instead of stone and many bow windows so that people could see the sea even if they were sideways on to it. The only seaside town, besides Brighton with its oriental pavilion, which went in for rival attractions to the water in a really expensive way was Devonport, whose Greek Town Hall, lofty columns, Egyptian Forester's Hall and the, alas demolished, Turkish Hall beside it formed the centre of a place which was once and yet may still be more important than the more squalid Plymouth which tried to absorb it.

Follies – they are today regarded as something expensive, ridiculous and not needed. I doubt if the word when used in the sense of a tower or a monument to catch the eye is even connected with the word foolish. I think it is far more likely to be connected with the French word *feuille* meaning a leaf. I think it originally stood for clumps of leafy trees to be seen at the end of a street, as you see Beechen Cliff, Bath, from the Royal Circus, or as you see clumps of oak, elm or beech from the terrace of an old country house when you look out across the park to seeming endlessness beyond.

The woods and coverts on English downs and hills, even the clumps of trees in flat landscape, are what used to be called follies. It is to the folly of previous generations who planted these places with an eye to the future that we are indebted today. In the same way we are indebted to previous generations, from the Middle Ages to the Victorian, for preserving the vistas at the ends of streets in our towns. The only enemies of follies are 'developers'.

In his mind he belongs to an unhurried and polite age

Verse, Fiction and Musings Miscellaneous

ഇ൯

Although reviews and architecture formed the bulk of Betjeman's writing for the *Telegraph* publications, there were times, particularly when he wrote for the magazine, when he provided very different kinds of articles. The occasion of Sir Max Beerbohm's 80th birthday engendered a personal tribute, whilst Christmas editions of the magazine saw him contribute, along with others, to wider features, one year producing a ghost story. There was even poetry such as the somewhat cheerless 'Meditation on the A30' and a curious 'hedge poem' on the Irish town of Trim. Rounded up here is just about everything outside of reviews and architectural articles that Betjeman contributed to the newspaper in the fifties and sixties, closing with his fantasy about an Australian island which neatly sums up the themes of his *Telegraph* writings up in a nutshell.

Sir Max Beerbohm:
An 80th Birthday Tribute

23 August 1952

ℬℭ

I t is pleasant to be asked to send him a birthday present. It is pleasant to think that these words may meet his eyes tomorrow. There, on the front steps of the villa in Rapallo, among the empty Chianti battles or whatever it is that one puts outside an Italian villa for the equivalent of the milkman to collect, may be lying this morning's *Daily Telegraph*.

Its familiar pages will be bleaching in the Mediterranean sun. Someone will carry it up to a tidy room whose French windows open on a terrace. And on that terrace he will be sitting looking down over olives and cypress trees to the 'wrinkled sea' below. Between sea and him the motor horns will be hooting along the road from Genoa to Viareggio which passes below his villa. Noise of internal combustion engines will not disturb him.

Unhurried and Polite

As in his mind he belongs to an unhurried and polite age, so does he in his body. There will be none of that giving in to the heat with open collar and vulgar summer colours you can see at any English seaside resort. He will be correctly and coolly dressed in the sober shades we often see in his caricatures, pale greys and blues.

And his dress, his slow, courteous speech, his quiet way of life are all part of that age around 1910 when he first came to live at Rapallo; the English exquisite, the calm perfectionist, famous then, even more famous today.

Sense of Proportion

I suppose what he has better than all the rest of us is a sense of proportion. He can see the ridiculous in everything, so he never loses his temper. He never hates. The nearest he comes to hate is pity. It is this sense of proportion which gives him those polite manners. You can hear them even in the model letter he wrote on 'How to thank author for inscribed copy of book' from *And Even Now*:

> Dear Mr Emanuel Flower — It was kind of you to think of sending me a copy of your new book. It would have been kinder still to think again and abandon that project. I am a man of gentle instincts and do not like to tell you that *A Flight Into Arcady* (of which I have skimmed a few pages, thus wasting two or three minutes of my not altogether worthless time) is trash.
>
> On the other hand, I am determined that you shall not be able to go around boasting to your friends, if you have any, that this work was not condemned, derided and dismissed by your sincere well-wisher, Wrexford Cripps.

You can hear those good manners, too, in the French café in his story about the millionaire
J.L. Pethel from *Seven Men*:

> ... squaring his arms on the little table he asked me what I would drink. I protested that I was the host — a position which he, with the quick courtesy of the very rich, yielded to me at once.

A sense of proportion is the basis of all true humour. If it overbalances into anger, humour becomes satire. There is very little satire in Max Beerbohm. His rare wrath is righteous. He takes no pleasure in the knockabout and the pun. His phantasy, as in *Zuleika*

Dobson and those even better stories in *Seven Men* – 'Enoch Soames' and 'Maltby and Braxton' – is that of the fairy tale and ghost story.

It was his sense of proportion, too, which made him so distinguished a dramatic critic in his early days, when he wrote weekly for the *Saturday Review* for twelve years. One can read those criticisms in the rare collected edition and laugh oneself silly over ham acting in plays one has never seen nor will ever hear of again.

And what other gifts, besides this great one of proportion, have been given him to use these eighty years? Next most prominent is that ear for prose. He can imitate anyone. He can imitate almost too well. I believe that the only author who was offended among those parodied in 'A Christmas Garland' was A.C. Benson, whose 'From a College Window' he pilloried in 'Out of Harm's Way'. Do you remember the closing lines of that parody?:

> A singular repose, a sense of security, an earnest of calm and continuity, as though he were reading over again one of those wise copybooks that he had so loved in boyhood, or were listening to the sounds made on a piano by some modest, very conscientious young girl, with a pale red pigtail, practising her scales, very gently, hour after hour, next door.

One can hardly blame A.C. Benson for being offended.

Eye for Detail

And the other prominent gift is his eye for colour and detail. You can see it in that pale red pigtail. You can see it better in any of the caricatures. He notices dress as much as faces – the carelessly tied tie, the crease in the right place, the bulge in the wrong one.

The man endowed with such a highly developed sense of the ridiculous as Max usually becomes a cynic. To that temptation he has not yielded. He is 'tough', a word he would not like me to use about him and I hope he will forgive it.

But, heaven knows, there must have been temptations. He makes no bones about his opinion of this century or the common man. He says he is much looking forward to the year 2000.

There are probably many men in chambers off Piccadilly, in the two remaining private rooms of their country houses, who have lapsed into cynicism or despair. For they, too, have known the London Max knew – the gaslights, Queen Victoria on the throne, puffed sleeves, bicycling in Battersea Park, riding in the Row, silly beauties in picture hats, aesthetes in velvet. Port, cigars and unamalgamated railways.

There can be none who knew so many of the intellectual and famous of the time. If they did, they have not left so much written or pictorial record of it.

We come back to that sense of proportion. Charterhouse, Oxford, a sound knowledge of Latin and Greek, a little French and presumably some Italian, a gift for drawing and writing: no 'deep' stuff, no Russian novelists, nothing abstract, no economics, philosophy and politics – Max has always kept within his range. He does what interests him, and he describes things he loves, and he uses all his talents all the time.

A Letter of Thanks

Max knew a civilised people. For he lived in civilised circles in London. He has determined to keep it alive in himself and in his art, the little part of it he knew, which happens to be a very interesting part.

He has achieved it in himself, sitting there on the terrace at Rapallo.

He has put them down, those last thirty years before the collapse of civilisation in 1910. It is in his books and drawings, which I can reread and look at again and again because they are skilful, truthful, inspired and affectionate. By identifying himself with the period to which he belongs Max Beerbohm is making himself immortal.

This, which should have been a birthday present and sounds unpleasantly like an obituary, is, I see, really a letter of thanks.

***

Exhibition of Decorative Art

24 October 1952

୫୦ ଓଃ

Today the Victorian and Edwardian Exhibition at the Victoria and Albert Museum will be opened to the public. The private view took place yesterday. It opens the eyes. The first thing that strikes one is the courage of those glorious ages.

There is no rot about pastel shades and self-conscious 'restraint'. Think of our modern lack of interest in what we see in houses and offices. I doubt if there is a single person reading these words who will not go into a room somewhere today which is coloured that inevitable government department cream, or else nursing-home green.

Pictures on the walls will be few and what is known as choice, thin pale oak frames surrounding reproductions of some safe Old Master or French impressionist. I wish that even a sixteenth of the money spent on reproductions today went instead to the purchasing for about three guineas to five guineas of original drawings by young struggling artists.

Sound Craftsmanship

But no, we leave our artists to the patronage of none too rich public galleries. We have not the courage of our own convictions. We know what we like and dare not admit we like it.

The art experts, the 'art historians', those new invaders, are sapping our confidence by cataloguing and pontificating, and thus they find jobs for themselves and their followers.

Everything in this exhibition, wallpaper, furniture, fabrics, tapestry, jewellery, altar frontals, china and glass, is obviously well made. I took the opportunity when no one was looking of sliding drawers; they did not stick: of opening cupboards they hung well: of treading on rugs and they were thick and rich.

Work was done thoroughly for the love of it. Craftsmanship today has gone away to motor cars, armaments and aeroplanes, except for a few notable exceptions.

Period Styles

Of course, as soon as it appears in a museum with a little label on it and a rope across, a piece of furniture dies and looks as sad as a butterfly pinned on a board. It looks doubly sad when it is from a room we ourselves knew, or something very like it.

What is a hefty oaken table in the Philip Webb and William Morris style without the earnest garden city freethinkers of King Edward's reign sitting round it and eating raw shredded cabbage and nuts?

What are tapering tables in white enamel and Art Nouveau panels on the walls without long ladies in white with opal and silver necklaces? The furniture and decorations need the people we knew who loved them.

But this exhibition stimulates the imagination. I could have wished that the authorities had spent some money on building contemporary rooms round the objects. One would have been able to appreciate the proportions of the furniture better, and the colour schemes. Then, they did not disdain bright scarlets and greens and golds. Any darkness they set off with white enamel paint on all woodwork.

But with their resources, the museum officials have produced a serious exhibition, although those giants of the Victorian age, George

Edmund Street and his pupil Norman Shaw, the greatest architect since Wren, are sadly under-represented, Street indeed not at all.

The exhibition will help to dispel the wrong impression that Victorian decoration was all wax fruit, tassels and sociables. There were various phases of Victorian and Edwardian decoration.

For your convenience when visiting the exhibition or looking round some old-fashioned room near where you live, I submit this general summary.

All 'research students' are welcome to write in angry corrections.

1840–70

Decoration still the perquisite of the wealthy; Tractarians liked lofty rooms; Gothic was popular; large bookcases and cupboards in varnished light oak; paintwork generally grained oak; walls with flock-papers in gold and scarlet or gold and royal blue; big historical pictures.

Alternative style to Gothic, flowery French classic, maple wood and gilt furniture, ironwork heating stoves, enamel let into woodwork, crystal gasoliers, glazed chintzes, wallpaper with naturalistic large bunches of roses or trellises of ivy; heavy meals.

Merchants, travelling by steam to suburbs like Edgbaston outside Birmingham, Sefton Park outside Liverpool, Highbury and Crystal Palace districts outside London, were fond of this style. Merchants' houses were usually Italianate and in white brick.

1870–90

Decoration percolating to the middle classes. Norman Shaw built red-brick houses in a Flemish style known as 'Queen Anne'; leaded panes or small wooden panes to windows; steep roofs; solid-looking chimney stacks.

Interiors rather dark with flat green or flat plum-coloured wainscot and woodwork, Morris wallpapers and some other stylised wallpapers. Prevailing colours brown and green. Dark oak furniture, preferably Elizabethan; William de Morgan tiles round the fireplace.

At Bedford Park, Chiswick, Norman Shaw laid out a suburb among old trees. It had winding roads, an inn, a co-operative store and a church. Small red-brick houses, each different yet each harmonising with its neighbour in Dutch style, scale and texture, were designed for artistic persons of moderate income.

Bedford Park, which still survives, is the mother of the English small house and of such experiments as Letchworth and Hampstead Garden Suburb.

1890–1910

A brief phase of 'Art Nouveau' invented in Glasgow; it was an escape from revivals and owes something to the current fashions of Japanese art. Long tenuous lines, white enamel paint, faint dashes of pale violet and green in stained glass and chintzes. The lift doors of some of the older London Underground stations are Art Nouveau. This Aubrey Beardsley Scottish Baronial style was loved by the Germans. They turned it into the frightful bogus-modern which has come back to us in super-cinemas and chain-store shopfronts.

From 1900 onwards was the great period of the small house, the Edwardian age's lasting and finest contribution to British architecture.

Names like Baillie Scott, Edgar Wood, Parker Unwin, Voysey, Rowntree and the Tugwells will one day be famous everywhere. Some of their work is shown here. They used local styles and materials and often themselves designed the chintzes, china and plate and furniture for their houses, in the simple William Morris tradition. We associate it with Arts and Crafts which we used to laugh at but now wish we possessed when plastic things break and drawers in modern suites won't open and green timber splits in the central heating.

At the end of the period, not shown in the exhibition, was a return to Sir Christopher Wren and baroque, much favoured for boardrooms and banks and liners.

Unrecognised Beauty

The Victorians and Edwardians are rather near to be given their due in architecture and decoration. Heaven forbid that this meritorious exhibition of much that is beautiful and interesting and unrecognised should breed yet one more school of 'experts'. But if it helps us to use our eyes and rescue forgotten craftsmanship from attics, cupboards, and junk shops, it will have done a great work.

The Victorians and Edwardians, like all civilised people, knew what they liked and were not afraid to show it. By comparison, we are cowards with our committee taste and lack of conviction in all but what is temporary.

At least the Victorians did not face the land with concrete lamp standards, poles and wires simply because they were cheap. They loved beauty, not cheapness, even though their idea of it was not always yours and mine.

***

Small Town of Ireland

21 January 1966

෨౪

Public houses in Irish country towns are often shops as well. You drink at a counter with bacon on it. Plastic dustpans hang from the ceiling. Over all is the delicious silence of Ireland. Among the notices pinned to the board, a ballad – called hedge poetry – might even be found. My ballad has been illustrated with photographs of Trim in County Meath. It does not directly refer to Trim, which must be one of the most romantic small towns in Britain, but it tries to give a view of those too little regarded places.

I have annotated it for English readers.

The small towns of Ireland by bards are neglected,
They stand there, all lonesome, on hilltop and plain.
The Protestant glebe house by beech trees protected
Sits close to the gates of his lordship's demesne.

But where is his lordship, who once in a phaeton
Drove out 'twixt his lodges and into the town?
Oh his tragic misfortunes I will not dilate on,
His mansion's a ruin, his woods are cut down.

His impoverished descendant is dwelling in Reading,
His daughters must type for their bread and their board,
O'er the graves of his forebears the nettle is spreading
And few will remember the sad Irish lord.

Yet still stands the mall where his agent resided,
The doctor, attorney and such class of men.
The elegant fanlights and windows provided
A Dublin-like look for the town's Upper Ten.

'Twas bravely they stood by the Protestant steeple
As over the town rose their roof-trees afar.

Let us slowly descend to the part where the people
Do mingle their ass-carts by Finnegan's bar.

I hear it once more, the soft sound of those voices,
When fair day is filling with farmers the square,
And the heart in my bosom delights and rejoices
To think of the dealing and drinking done there.

I see thy grey granite, oh grim House of Sessions!
I think of the judges who sat there in state
And my mind travels back to our monster processions
In honour of heroes of brave 'Ninety-Eight.

The barracks are burned where the Redcoats oppressed us,
The gaol is broke open, our people are free.
Though Cromwell once cursed us, Saint Patrick has blessed us,
The merciless English have fled o'er the sea.

Look out where yon cabins grow smaller to smallest,
Straw-thatched and one-storey and soon to come down
To where rises a steeple, the newest and tallest,
Of Saint Malachy's Catholic church in our town.

The fine architecture, the wealth of mosaic,
The various marbles on altars within –
To attempt a description were merely prosaic,
So, asking your pardon, I will not begin.

Oh, my small town of Ireland, the raindrops caress you,
The sun sparkles bright on your field and your square,
As here on your bridge I salute you and bless you
Your murmuring waters and turf-scented air.

A glebe house is the Irish name for a rectory. By Protestant, I mean Church of Ireland. In Trim, the Church of Ireland building has been elevated to a cathedral for the ancient diocese of Meath. It stands on the site of the Celtic church where St Patrick, who came from Britain, started his mission in the fifth century.

Unlike most Irish country towns, Trim has no big house belonging to a lord placed at its edge. The ruined house and park with obelisks which belonged to Lord Mornington, the father of Arthur Wesley (Wellesley), Duke of Wellington, is a few miles out of the town and called Dangan Castle. It is in the parish of Laracor, where Swift was rector. Wellington was educated in the school at Trim. Sir William Rowan Hamilton, the famous mathematician, was his fellow pupil. As a schoolboy, Wellington is said to have climbed the great Yellow Tower, 125 feet high. Before doing so, he left his belongings by will to some of the other boys. During his climb up to the top, Rowan Hamilton wept bitterly. When asked why, he said it was because Arthur had left him nothing. In 1817, the people of Meath erected a column to Wellington.

The mall is the name given to a terrace of Georgian houses in a small town. The better-off professional classes who lived in such houses often belonged to the Church of Ireland.

The Sessions House in Trim is a handsome classical building of about 1840, and is called the Courthouse. The Irish Republican Army burned down the barracks of the Royal Irish Constabulary in the town in 1920. As a reprisal, the Black and Tans (English soldiers) burned the Town Hall, so the Courthouse was the Town Hall until the new one was built.

'Ninety-Eight in the poem refers to the rebellion (1798) of the Irish under Wolfe Tone, a Protestant, the Lord Edward Fitzgerald, and Henry Joy McCracken in Ulster, against the English for oppressing the Catholics and not allowing Ireland to be governed by its own people.

An Irishman of Norman descent to whom I showed this ballad said that after 'The merciless English have fled o'er the sea' should be inserted:

> We still send them marshals and cattle and wheat
> And jockeys and poets and men for their wars,
> Which helps them to hold the whole world at their feet.
> For with such occupation they stay from our shores.

The Norman, later mediaeval, Elizabethan and Cromwellian families who lived in Ireland have bred our greatest soldiers, sailors and strategists — witness Wellington, Alexander, Montgomery.

Trim is on the western edge of the Pale, which is the part between Dublin and the west where, for 750 years, England practised for building an empire and Ireland provided the forces and the empire builders.

The tallest building in most Irish country towns is generally the Roman Catholic church. It represents in the Republic of Ireland about 95 per cent of the population, and the rich decorations of the churches, the schools and convents and monasteries have been paid for by the people. Until the middle of the last century no Roman Catholic church was allowed a tower or a spire. Hence the desire for rebuilding when permission was granted, and the large late Victorian and more recent Catholic churches.

***

Meditation on the A30

21 October 1966

౭౦౮౩

A man on his own in a car
Is revenging himself on his wife;
He opens the throttle and bubbles with dottle
And puffs at his pitiful life.

'She is losing her looks very fast,
She loses her temper all day:
That lorry won't let me get past
This Mini is blocking my way.

'Hell's bells! Hurry up! Make a move!
I can't go on dawdling like this!
At breakfast she said that she wished I was dead
And it's years since she gave me a kiss.

'I'd like a nice blonde on my knee
And one who won't argue or nag.

Who dares to come hooting at *me*?
I only give way to a Jag.

'You're barmy or plastered, I'll pass you, you bastard
I *will* overtake you. I *will!*'
As he clenches his pipe, his moment is ripe
And the corner's accepting its kill.

***

Haunted Stories for Christmas Firesides

Wrecker's Cave

22 December 1967

ࣟ

I must have been about ten years old when this happened. That is to say it was about 1916, and summer holidays in north Cornwall. It was a remote place then – oil lamps, farmhouse teas, few motor cars, and the London and South Western Railway crawling along its single line through Launceston to Wadebridge and Padstow. A wet silence hung over the nights, and legends survived as yet uncommercialised, and we were young enough to believe them. One of these was about a smuggler called Cruel Coppinger – Baring Gould writes of him in his romance *In the Roar of the Sea*. Coppinger lured ships to their doom on our great slate cliffs. When a ship was sighted he would wave a lantern so that her captain thought she was approaching harbour, but instead she was approaching a hostile cove near Port Isaac full of rocks. Coppinger arrived in the district mysteriously. It was said he was a Dane. Like another famous wrecker, Gilbert Mawgan, he is said to have left the sailors thrown up not quite dead, to die on the rocks. Mawgan even went so far as to bury alive the captain of a vessel whom he found exhausted on the strand. When Coppinger was dying – as when Mawgan died – there was a tremendous sea and a strange vessel came up channel from nowhere. On the wrecker's death it stood out to sea and disappeared.

Between two bays to which we used to make day expeditions on foot there ran a tunnel. At high tide, and even at half-tide, if you had been in this tunnel you would have been trapped. It was said that there was a way out of the tunnel by a shaft to the open air. Certainly, from the cliff path above, a dank cavern with luminous moss in it was said to lead down to the tunnel between the two bays. I never liked going down it myself because of the hole said to have been used by Cruel Coppinger for bringing up his plunder from the sea caves below.

One day bolder children than I, with me in their wake, explored the sea cave at a low spring tide in order to find the way through to the other bay. We wore bathing dresses. At first there was the usual scrambling over boulders and avoiding a slippery kind of green seaweed until it was too dark to know what sort of weeds, pools, or rocks were at our feet. The cave narrowed and I hoped it would peter out altogether so that we should have to turn back. But no. There was a pool in total darkness and the water came up to my chin. The others had gone ahead. I could still hear their voices. Then there was a sudden change in the air. Instead of the salt, seaweedy, iodine smell, it was as though I was in a stuffy much-breathed-in room. I had a distinct feeling, though I saw nothing, that there was someone else behind me who was not of our party. The rather sinister caress of what might have been ribbon weed, or a sea spider's legs, around my ankles made me swim forward, breast stroke, as hard as I could. Then there was the light from the other bay, the air changed back to its sea-freshness and we were all safely through.

That afternoon someone photographed us on the rocks below the entrance to the cave. When we were shown the photograph there appeared in the black entrance to the cave a face with a big moustache and a tricorn hat. This was not an illusion created by the rock formation because it was in the black darkness of the cave aperture. I can think of four people alive today who must remember that photograph.

When I go to the scene now it looks small and used and there is litter about and always people, instead of the desertion we remember. And of course I cannot be certain now, for it is fifty years ago, whether I didn't imagine that presence in the middle blackness *after* I had seen the photograph. All I am certain of is that the face I saw in the photograph was there, and that it was nobody we knew and rather larger than life.

***

John Betjeman's Kangaroo Island

5 January 1968

œœ

The most enjoyable surprise of my life was a visit to Australia. I was only there six weeks, and wished it could have been as many years. Among the thousands of places I didn't see was Kangaroo Island, off Adelaide, which looks, on the map, larger than the Isle of Wight and in an area enjoying an equable climate. I like to imagine what Kangaroo Island is like, although many people may tell me I am wrong and that it is a desert or penal colony.

Having the sea around gives a sense of security. There is an old fishing port in a sheltered fissure in the gigantic cliffs of the west coast where the seas are tremendous. The old port is so placed that no winds reach it. It is famous for shellfish, enormous and very cheap local oysters, mussels and cockles and delicate prawns. Another town is on the milder, more tropical north coast. It consists of a stucco crescent and a square, not unlike a miniature

Brighton, and the gardens are varied by palms, fuchsias, magnolias and mimosa. It is sheltered from the prevailing wind by the mountainous country in the interior of the island where no conifers grow. The interior is partly unexplored, and hidden cities may be buried there.

The capital is in the southern part of the island, slightly inland and on a river. It is stone-built and the public buildings like the art gallery, the theatre and library and museum display the wide variety of local building stone-slate, granite and limestone. There is also a street of local brick looking rather like a Dutch picture where the doctors live and the solicitors.

Communication between these three towns should be by narrow-gauge steam railways whose rolling stock is at once highly coloured and comfortable. Services are frequent and punctual. No motor cars or motor bicycles or lorries should exist on this island. In the towns the roads are cobbled, which deters bicyclists from using them. Pedestrians are always in the right. From the end of every street you can see the country. I would like to think that there are electric tram cars to the two suburbs of the capital. One of these suburbs has a splendid church built by Butterfield in 1852, making full use of local materials. It was built 'High Church' and always has been. The other suburb of the town was built about 1890 by admirers of the 'simple life' and has cottage-style houses rather like Hampstead Garden Suburb, built of mellow brick and local stone. The church here is a cathedral of the Arts and Crafts movement. Its pews are of adzed unstained oak. Its electroliers are like magnified Art Nouveau jewellery and its stained glass is a dark, rich purple and red, enlivened with gold. In this suburb there is an excellent vegetarian restaurant.

The island has advantages for people of less specialised tastes. There should be no licensing hours, no breathalysers (these are not necessary, because of the absence of the motor car), and of course there is no tax on drink or tobacco. Pleasure is a virtue and the enjoyment of life is not a vice. There are, therefore, several theatres and a great many cinemas. The island is unique in its extensive library of first-class films dating back to the silent film. There is every sort of golf course, natural, park-like and miniature. There are two racecourses, one flat and one with fences, and the trainers may be found in the varied farmland in the centre of the island. There are no newspapers and no critics. What news there is, is promulgated by the town crier, and it is all good. There is a flourishing local school of artists and craftsmen.

Litter and playing transistor sets in quiet places are crimes. Speed is a crime. But the greatest crime is priggery, that is to say, thinking you are better than somebody else, intellectually, morally or racially.

As this island is Anglican there is no persecution of any other religions. Hospitals are places where you can live until you die. People are so glad to live on this island that they willingly pay taxes because they are a tribute of thanksgiving and not an extortion to pay for other people's ideas.

The Reality

There are kangaroos on Kangaroo Island — and wallabies, seals, emus, opossums, platypuses, koalas and 2,000 or more human residents. This ninety-miles-long island lies six hours from Port Adelaide by a twice-weekly drive-on, drive-off ferry, or only forty minutes by the daily air service (cars can be hired).

Accommodation needs to be booked in advance, though development is under way to cater for the swell in population in summer, when temperatures are a welcome six to eight degrees cooler than on the mainland. But today it is still essentially unspoilt.

The taste by which
he was relished
Obituary

ରେ ଙ

John Betjeman died on Saturday 19 May 1984 at his home in Trebetherick, Cornwall, aged seventy-seven. For twenty-four consecutive years of his life he had supplied articles for the *Daily Telegraph*, reviewing around a thousand books and writing numerous other articles. Yet strangely his obituary in the newspaper, which covered most of page 3 on the issue of 21 May, mentioned none of this. As the *Telegraph* did not have the dedicated obituaries department it has today, fellow poet Philip Larkin was commissioned to write the appreciation of the newspaper – perhaps he wasn't aware of Betjeman's long-running connection? The leader article to mark the writer's passing also concentrated on Betjeman the poet rather than the columnist, but his contribution to newsprint hadn't gone entirely unremarked – the front-page story on his death in the previous day's *Sunday Telegraph*, with the curious headline SECRETARY SAVED BETJEMAN LINES, mentioned it in the section of the article about the poet's life, before speculating as to who would be his successor as Poet Laureate; stating 'There is no obvious heir apparent', but presciently mentioning Ted Hughes amongst the possible candidates. So, to end this book, we reprint Larkin's appreciation of a man who over three decades enriched the pages of the *Telegraph* with his many reviews and articles, and in so doing did much to highlight the enduring worth of so many lovely bits of old England.

Betjeman, From Obscurity to TV Stardom

Philip Larkin

21 May 1984

ဆဝၺ

The death at seventy-seven of the Poet Laureate, Sir John Betjeman, takes from English poetry its most original figure and from English life a widely known and much-loved personality.

Not since Tennyson has a Laureate enjoyed such national renown, for in addition to his reputation as a poet Betjeman won fame as a writer on architecture, pioneer conservationist, social historian and television entertainer.

Yet his success contained an element of paradox.

At the beginning of his career in the early nineteen thirties, he was known only to a small circle as a passionate devotee of the obscure and unfashionable in architecture and literature, and as the author of poems that exhibited (to quote a contemporary review) 'bourgeois taste at its most corrupt'.

By the end of his life, however, he commanded audiences of millions for his television programmes on these same, individual interests, while his *Collected Poems* (1978) had brought him a degree of popularity previously associated with Kipling, Brooke and Housman.

Truly he had created, as Wordsworth said all great and original writers must, the taste by which he was relished.

Poetic Revolution Unrecognised

Sir John (he was knighted in 1969) was indeed something of an anomaly among twentieth-century poets: for him, the poetic revolution of Pound, Eliot and their successors had simply not taken place. Equally, he was resolutely opposed to the spirit of the age: never was a poet less likely to 'look shining at new styles of architecture' or welcome the dictatorship of the proletariat.

Yet at the same time his work was intensely contemporary, celebrating the remnants of the past along with the more egregious manifestations of the present; everything, in fact, that made up his subject matter of:

> Dear old, bloody old England
> Of telegraph poles and tin ...

and by its very nature came to constitute an unofficial alternative to 'modern poetry' as taught in schools and universities.

Popular Choice as Laureate

His appointment to the Laureateship in 1972 was a popular choice, and its honour well deserved. It was not to be expected that so personal a poet would excel in the production of public verse (although his poem on the investiture of the Prince of Wales represented an adroit marriage of style and subject), but his readings on radio and television did much to bring to numerous listeners poems they might not otherwise have encountered.

Betjeman's name became a household word for sensibility that could respond equally to the cities of Australia and old London street lamps. All this was done with unqualified enthusiasm and modestly worn learning that proclaimed that beauty of a place or period, building or word was not a professional mystery but the property of anyone with eyes to see or ears to hear.

Born in 1906, John Betjeman was the only child of Ernest Edward Betjeman, a manufacturer of domestic furnishings such as the 'Betjeman Tantalus'. In *Summoned by Bells* (1960), a sharply detailed blank-verse account of his childhood and youth, he describes his schooldays at Highgate School, Dragon School, Oxford and Marlborough College, and makes clear his father's disappointment at his own unwillingness to succeed him in the family business.

A Reluctant Schoolboy

In many ways a reluctant schoolboy, by the time he went to Magdalen College in 1925 Betjeman had laid the foundations of his lifelong love of the architecture of the eighteenth and nineteenth centuries (not to mention their minor poets), and Maurice Bowra, then a young don at Wadham College, was surprised by the extent of his knowledge and the originality of his mind.

His own tutor, C.S. Lewis, was less impressed, but although Betjeman went down in 1928 without taking a degree (he failed Divinity Moderations) he had by that time confirmed his allegiance to his own special interests, and made enduring friendships among what was an exceptionally brilliant Oxford generation. His affectionate regard for Oxford itself was demonstrated in *An Oxford University Chest* (1938), and in 1973 the University conferred on him an honorary doctorate.

Betjeman's ruling passion for the churches, country houses and public buildings of the last two centuries led to an early appointment as assistant editor of *The Architectural Review*, and was entertainingly exemplified in *Ghastly Good Taste* (1933), the first of a long series of books, such as the Shell Guides, devoted to expounding the beauties of buildings and places, a task for which he had an unsurpassed talent.

Without claiming to be an art historian in any conventional sense, he could summon an immediate warmth for almost every kind of building, and show how its designers had instinctively exhibited qualities of proportion and taste seemingly lost to their twentieth-century successors. In fact it was to this kind of appreciation that Betjeman devoted his considerable energies.

He wrote very little about literature as such, but his definition of architecture was a wide one: 'your surroundings; not a town or street, but our whole over-populated island', and extended into the vicissitudes of social behaviour and what today would be called environmental studies.

Underneath his high-spirited mockery of church restorers, property developers and municipal planners lay a deep concern for the quality of communal life as shown by what we build and, even more, what we knock down. 'Almost any age,' he wrote, 'seems civilised except that in which I live.'

A Force for Conservation

Since the war his signature was constantly to be found under letters appealing for the preservation of buildings as diverse as the Coal Exchange, Euston Arch, the Imperial Institute and Marx House, as well as others protesting against the proposed road through Christ Church Meadows and Stansted Airport. This never-sleeping concern brought him membership of the Royal Commission on Historical Monuments, and the Royal Institute of British Architects made him an honorary associate in 1957.

Betjeman's love of church architecture, best exemplified in *Collins Guide to English Parish Churches* (1958) with its long and beautiful introduction, was bound up with the history of the Church of England and a feeling for its ritual:

> The steps to truth were made by sculptured stone,
> Stained glass and vestments, holy-water stoups,
> Incense and crossings of myself ...

Many of his early poems rejoiced in the nuances of sectarianism and Nonconformity, but paradoxically this never blinded him to broader issues. 'Highness or lowness does not matter. You are the Church, and must not scatter,' he wrote in the deceptively light *Poems in the Porch* (1954) and in *Summoned by Bells*:

What seemed to me a greater question then
Tugged and still tugs: Is Christ the Son of God?

Television Personality

Throughout his life an active member of the Church of England (he was Governor of Pusey House, where as an undergraduate he used to worship), Betjeman's poetic declarations of faith were nevertheless often equivocal ('And is it true? For if it is ...'). Despite his high-spirited relish for life and his growing success as a writer, his nature was flawed by a lack of self-confidence ('frequent sackings gave me a sense of failure and insecurity') and a dread of death that he struggled against but honestly refused to minimise. This basic spiritual uncertainty increased the appeal of his poems to an age that had lost the faith to which he clung.

The nationwide fame that he eventually achieved, however, came predominantly from his success as a television personality. Early appearances on panel programmes (as when identifying buildings in *Where on Earth?*) had brought into play his engaging unselfconsciousness and remarkable specialised knowledge. Producers were quick to realise his potential as an individual performer.

Programmes in which Betjeman displayed his talent for introducing a place or a kind of building were immediately successful: London's railway stations, country houses, Wren churches and St Bartholomew's Hospital were all presented with an informed informality that was plainly without didactic intention but which left the viewer eager to learn more.

The most memorable of them, *Metro-land* (1973), was an exquisite visual and verbal celebration of the residential suburbs of London, Harrow, Pinner and Ruislip, that had so often figured in his poems.

Notwithstanding his natural gifts as a television performer, Betjeman made light of the reputation it brought him. 'I will be completely forgotten five years from now,' he said in 1961, adding that he valued the medium only insofar as it enabled him to show the beauties and intricacies of architecture to millions of viewers, and to make personal contact with different kinds of people while doing so.

Inevitably the reputation became something of a caricature – the hats, the teddy bear, the avuncular eccentricity – but Betjeman used it to disarm his audience with laughter so that they should be more receptive to the vision and values he was seeking to impart.

In this sense Betjeman was a lifelong propagandist; he constantly opposed bureaucratic officialdom, government indifference and commercial vulgarity and continually defended the spirit of art and literature against the letter of pedantry and jargon. This required considerable resilience and despite his public image Betjeman had sufficient qualities of toughness and even pugnacity to enable him to pursue his independent course.

Except during the war (when he served as UK Press Attaché in Dublin and later with the Admiralty and British Council) he earned his living as a freelance writer and broadcaster, an uncertain career needing more energy and resourcefulness to sustain than the conventional curatorship or chair.

Full Expression in His Poetry

Nevertheless it was in his poems that Betjeman's many faceted character received its full expression. It is for them that he will be remembered.

His first two books, *Mount Zion* (1935) and *Continental Dew* (1937) were unashamedly frivolous in format: differently coloured pages, photographs and engravings quarried from obscure sources, ornaments and emblems all proclaimed a mood greatly at odds with the temper of the thirties. Even the more decorous *Old Lights in New Chancels* (1940) still carried, with its paper labels, an affectation of Victorianism that was continued in *Old Bats in New Belfries* (1945) and was equally incongruous in a wartime economy.

Yet all these collections contained under their teasing exteriors poems of remarkable imagination and deep feeling, some of which

— though not, curiously, the most characteristic — had begun to appear in anthologies.

W.H. Auden and John Sparrow respectively edited selections in America (1947) and England (1948) but it was not until the publication of *A Few Late Chrysanthemums* (1954) that Betjeman began to attract readers outside his own immediate circle of admirers.

Success Came as a Surprise

Even so, the phenomenal success of *Collected Poems* in 1958 came as a complete surprise to author, publisher and public alike. Initially selling at the rate of 1,000 copies a week, it soon reached its first 100,000, and continued in a succession of revised editions in both hard cover and paperback. In 1960 Betjeman was awarded the Queen's Gold Medal for Poetry, and made a Commander of the Order of the British Empire.

The subjects of his poems were often idiosyncratic: church architecture, sports girls, death, his own childhood, the aged and the lonely, niceties of social habit ('Phone for the fish-knives, Norman'), English landscapes and localities, but the vigour he brought to them created a poetry of immediate response that with its exact rhyming and emphatic metres captured the reader even against his will.

Conversational Blank Verse

Betjeman's stanza forms were sometimes borrowed from favourite authors such as Praed and Barnes, sometimes completely original (as in the unusual yet deeply moving elegy on Walter Ramsden), and his own kind of conversational blank verse; in this, as in so much else, he ran quite counter to the fashions of his time.

Whereas Pound, Eliot, Auden, Empson and Dylan Thomas had exhibited varying kinds of obscurity that contemporary criticism had come to accept as essential ingredients of modern verse, Betjeman maintained the older tradition of direct communication with the reader in unambiguous language, and in doing so showed a vast public still existed for it.

Perhaps in consequence, critical opinion on his ultimate standing as a poet has been far from unanimous. Most writers have allowed him excellence as a maker of light verse with the occasional ability to touch deeper emotions, but they have been reluctant to place him alongside poets of a more consistently serious purpose, such as Eliot, Auden or Dylan Thomas.

Such a view hardly does justice to the ease with which his poems range from uproarious comedy to delicate pathos and ruthless honest, nor to his totally original vision of 'human topography'.

Luxuriance of Detail

The first poem in his first book, 'Death in Leamington', demonstrated this unique capacity to see people in terms of places, and places in terms of people, a gift that was deployed with infinite variety — comically, tenderly, satirically and with a luxuriance of Tennysonian details — throughout his whole corpus.

His simultaneous awareness of the social circumstances of human life and its poignant transience made him a superb chronicler of his time, producing poems of enduring quality such as 'Middlesex', 'Christmas', 'A Subaltern's Love Song' and 'The Metropolitan Railway', and this achievement may hold more lasting significance than was recognised in his lifetime.

While his death will be for many the loss of an irreplaceable friend, and for the nation the disappearance of a warm and invigorating personality, his work will remain as a memorial of twentieth-century English life refracted through a talent at once simple and complex, humorous and humble, linked with a heart of great feeling and total sincerity.